JEFF COOPER
THE ART OF THE
RIFLE

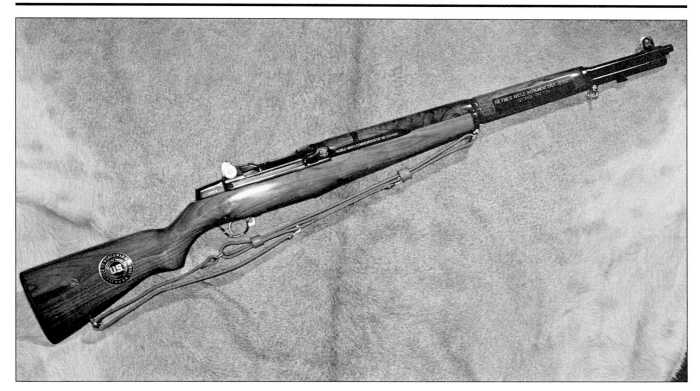

PALADIN PRESS · BOULDER, COLORADO

Also by Jeff Cooper:
Art of the Rifle (Special Color Edition)
C-Stories
Fireworks
Jeff Cooper's Defensive Pistolcraft Tape Series
Principles of Personal Defense
To Ride, Shoot Straight, and Speak the Truth

The Art of the Rifle
by Jeff Cooper

Copyright © 1997 by Jeff Cooper

ISBN 13: 978-1-58160-592-1
Printed in the United States of America

Published by Paladin Press, a division of
Paladin Enterprises, Inc.,
P.O. Box 1307
Boulder, Colorado 80306 USA
+1.303.443.7250

Direct inquiries and/or orders to the above address.

Most photos by Robert Anderson, Robert Anderson Photography, Phoenix, Arizona

The demonstrator in the illustrations is Giles Stock, repeat student of Jeff Cooper and rangemaster at Orange Gunsite.

Visit our website at www.paladin-press.com.

TABLE OF CONTENTS

1

THE QUEEN

Personal weapons are what raised mankind out of the mud, and the rifle is the queen of personal weapons. The possession of a good rifle, as well as the skill to use it well, truly makes a man the monarch of all he surveys. It realizes the ancient dream of the Jovian thunderbolt, and as such it is the embodiment of personal power. For this reason it exercises a curious influence over the minds of most men, and in its best examples it constitutes an object of affection unmatched by any other inanimate object.

The rifle has not been with us long—something on the order of 200 years—and it has been available to us in its modern form for just one short century. This passing 20th century can be characterized in one sense as the time of the rifle, because while the weapons used by George Washington and Daniel Boone were totally unlike the Mausers of the Boer War, those same Mausers are just as useful today as they were at the turn of the century. I have in my armory a Krag rifle, whose year of manufacture was 1892. It will do everything asked of it a hundred years later, and do it as well as anything available today. Thus the rifle, more than any other artifact, may be held up as the symbol of things as they ought to be, the ultimate instrument by which man has become master of his environment.

The rifle is a *weapon*. Let there be no mistake about that. It is a tool of power, and thus dependent completely upon the moral stature of its user. It is equally useful in securing meat for the table, destroying group enemies on the battlefield, and resisting tyranny. In fact, it is the only means of resisting tyranny, because a citizenry armed with rifles simply cannot be tyrannized.

The rifle itself has no moral stature, since it has no will of its own. Naturally, it may be used by evil men for evil purposes, but there are more good men than evil, and while the latter cannot be persuaded to the path of righteousness by propaganda, they can certainly be corrected by good men with rifles.

At this point in history, we have about reached the summit of our knowledge of the techniques of riflecraft—the art of the rifle. Fewer and fewer people are in a position to understand this art, due to the urbanization of the world and the increasing emasculation of mankind. Hence, it is time that the art of the rifle should be set forth as now understood, lest something very important be lost. While it is true that there exists in most nations a sport of rifle shooting, the formalization and specialization of target shooting competition has led its practitioners somewhat astray, in much the same way that the sporting practice of fencing has obscured the art of the sword.

The armed forces of today have almost abandoned the idea of serious riflecraft. There are many reasons for this, not the least of which is that rifle mastery is a demanding discipline and thus not really applicable to mass armies. There are other reasons. In an urban society it is doubtful whether a majority of young people have ever held a rifle in their hands, much less devoted themselves to its skillful use. Hunters, of course, shoot rifles, but hunting itself is imperiled in this tiresome age, and surely just because a man goes hunting does not mean that he knows how to use a rifle.

Probably the most serious obstacle to the popular understanding of riflecraft is the fact that rifle marksmanship is dependent entirely upon individual self-control, and self-control is out of fashion in the Age of the Common Man.

This book is about rifle shooting, rather than about rifles themselves. There have been many excellent technical works devoted to the evolution, structure, and design of rifles, but far fewer ones concerned with what a shooter does with the rifle when he has it. Rifle marksmanship is a somewhat simpler effort than playing a musical instrument, but it is not so simple as to be achieved without effort. "Nothing to it. You just point it and pull the trigger," was the old wheeze. This is rather like saying that all you have to do to play the piano well is to hit the right keys at the right time.

The various modes in which the rifle may be used will depend upon particular circumstances. The soldier has objectives that are different from those of the hunter, and the hunter of the ibex has goals different from the hunter of the leopard. Nevertheless, the principles of good shooting remain constant, embodied in the ability to cause the cartridge to explode at an instant when the sights are exactly on target.

In the days of my youth, the subject of rifle marksmanship was approached step-by-step. The first was sighting and aiming. The second was the firing position. The third was trigger control. And the fourth was rapid fire. I think this progression of steps is still valid, and we may proceed somewhat along these well-established lines. However, there is another element that was not covered back then but should be mentioned here: If the shooter does not cherish his weapon and feel sensual pleasure in handling it, it is unlikely that he will ever make it perform as efficiently as it can. This is one reason why armed organizations almost never shoot really well: The public servant has not the opportunity to fall in love with his piece if he must simply pluck it out from a number of similar items in a rack.

As Rudyard Kipling put it:

> "When half of your bullets fly wide in the ditch,
>   Don't call your Martini a cross-eyed old bitch,
>   She's human as you are; you treat her as sitch,
>   And she'll fight for the young British soldier."

On one occasion when St. George Littledale, the renowned British hunter of the "Roof of the World," showed his Tadjik scout the finely crafted piece he had brought from England, the latter inspected it lovingly, sighed deeply, and breathed, "And just to think—even the man who made this must die!"

There is an enchantment cast upon any woman when she holds a baby, whether or not it is her own. Similarly, there is an enchantment cast upon almost any man when he holds a rifle in his hands. This magical spell is both intellectual and emotional. Intellectually and emotionally, a rifle is a fascinating artifact, and its concept, design, and fabrication may be approached scientifically. A firearm may be "the simplest form of internal combustion engine," as the grease monkeys who used to live below decks on the warships of the past said. Nonetheless, the endless complexities involved in building a good rifle can absorb a hobbyist almost forever. The end product of these cogitations may be either a useful tool or a work of art. It is seldom both, as we see in the elaborate, bejeweled presentation pieces that collectors hang upon their walls. That is not to say that a rifle may not be both beautiful and efficient, but in my opinion efficiency comes first, and beauty of design will follow.

Elaborate finishing, with its engraving and inlay, may be a source of pride, but it does nothing to make the rifle a more efficient instrument. People are sometimes confused by

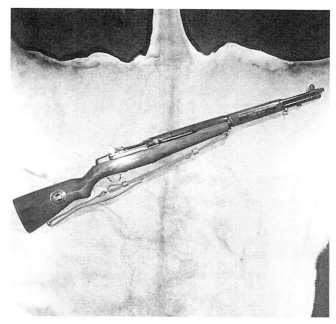

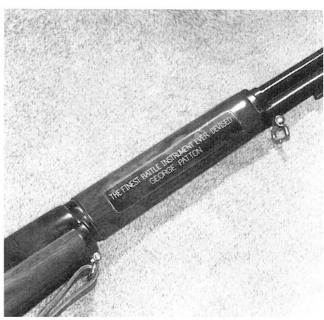

The M1 Garand.

this, and I once saw a weapon featured on a magazine cover that was extolled by its maker as the finest rifle in the world. It was far from that, though it was indeed pretty. Among its failures was the fact that it was not fitted with sights.

The other side of the coin that makes up the

joy of rifle handling is emotional, not scientific. Pick up a rifle—a really good rifle—and if you know how to use it well, you change instantly from a mouse to a man, from a peon to a *caballero*, and—most significantly—from a subject to a citizen. This is heady stuff and must be observed with circumspection. As Lord Acton put it, "Power tends to corrupt," and the rifle is the instrument of power. Handle it carefully. Learn to use it well. Make it part of you and you will have moved onto a superior plane of manhood.

Of course, not everyone feels this way, and there are many people who buy and sell rifles as a pastime of its own. To me, however, dealing in rifles is rather like dealing in human beings. A moral man may give away his treasures, but probably he should not sell them. Thus it is that at my advanced age I seek to find appreciative comrades who will provide good homes for my treasured rifles, but I will accept no money for them. The Queen is not for sale.

2
WHY?

In teaching rifle marksmanship, I have always opened the session by asking the students just why anyone should want to learn to shoot a rifle well. I never ask for a direct answer, since such matters are very personal, but I call upon the student to answer the question to himself: "Why do I want to learn to shoot a rifle?"

- *"To defend myself."* The rifle is not a defensive tool conceptually, though it has upon occasion been put to defensive use, but self-defense is not a convincing answer to this question.
- *"To fight my country's battles in the field."* This answer is better, but not entirely satisfactory. Today's battles are fought only sketchily with individual arms, and these arms change from year to year. So while a uniformed soldier should, in truth, know how to handle the weapon he is issued, student motivation in these cases is not conspicuously evident.
- *"To be able to acquit myself properly in the hunting field."* This is a good reason, but of decreasing significance in an age when fewer and fewer people go hunting. Those who do understand the hunting passion should naturally seek to use their weapons well, but really superior marksmanship is only occasionally the attribute of a hunter.
- *"Because I wish to win shooting matches."* This is

another good reason, and the social aspect of competitive shooting is considerable. Not long ago a girl who had conspicuous success in international rifle competition told an interviewer that the reason she went out for rifle shooting was because "that was where the boys were." Good enough!

- *"Because it is fun!"* Very well, but then we must ask, *why* it is fun? Well, it is challenging. Any challenge to which one submits himself is attractive to a great many people—witness golf. But many things are challenging, from checkers to Frisbee, and while these activities are enjoyable, they do not furnish the satisfaction that comes to a really good rifle shot.

This, I believe, is because the rifle is a tool of power. A good rifleman can bring kinetic power to bear upon his environment. He can reach out and cause things to happen decisively and selectively at a distance. With a good rifle in his hand, and the skill to use it well, he becomes, in a sense, a godlike figure. He may not need to use this power, but he commands it, and this is inexpressibly gratifying. This will to power is viewed askance by many who may be described as overcivilized. They hold that a man should not wish to command power, but whether he should or not is irrelevant, since he does. It is futile to tell a man he should choose to be helpless when he should be taught how to use the power that he can command wisely and well. So, we have rifle shooting. At least some of us have, at least in the 20th century. God alone knows what will become of this art in the 21st.

WHO IS A GOOD SHOT?

The more one considers the subject, the more difficult it becomes to define good marksmanship. On the wall of the classroom at Old Gunsite, we used to display the following inscription:

A marksman is one who can make his weapon do what it was designed to do.

An expert marksman is one who can hit anything he can see, under appropriate circumstances.

A master marksman is one who can shoot up to his rifle.

This is a point of departure. The Pennsylvania deer hunter who invariably tags out on opening day shoots well enough to make his weapon do what it was designed to do. So is the African professional hunter who never fails to stop a charge. So was the U.S. Marine captain who killed seven Japanese soldiers with eight shots on Saipan. And so is the Olympian who takes the gold in the rifle match.

The expert rifleman is one who can hit anything he can see. Perhaps we could say the person who can hit any appropriate target he can see, since clearly he can see the moon, but he cannot hit it with his rifle. The substance of this position was brought home to me many years ago after a rifle match in California wherein my middle daughter had just taken first place in an informal big-bore rifle match with no restrictions upon age or gender. After people had finished congratulating her, she spoke to me as she put her weapon away, "I don't know what the fuss is about, Daddy. If I can see it, I can hit it." I have always held this observation up as an example of how the rifleman should think.

The master rifleman is a man who can shoot up to his rifle. That means he can eliminate human error and place his bullets within the mechanical limitations of his weapon. This consideration has no reference to bench-rest shooting. The shooting bench is designed to eliminate human error, and whether it does or not, it is not a measure of marksmanship. The man whose shot groups, fired from field positions unsupported, match those he fires off the bench may be called a master marksman. We do not encounter him often.

When we examine the exploits of legendary riflemen, we run into trouble stemming from inaccurate reporting and the human tendency to "improve the story." Obviously, what one man did once is no measure of his skill. *It is what he can do upon demand that counts.* The famed shot by Billy Dixon at Adobe Walls is a good example of this. Dixon was observed to take that Comanche off his horse with one round at the fantastic distance of 1,348 yards. There was no possible way to make an accurate assessment of bullet drop at that distance—besides which, that target could not be seen with any clarity. Dixon himself afterwards clearly stated that he simply took a chance and lucked out, but his admirers attributed that to mere modesty, and the reputation as the world's finest marksman has clung to him ever since.

W.D.M. Bell, of Karamojo fame, was widely held to be "the finest shot in Africa," because of his astonishing record of one-shot elephant kills, using light but penetrative rifles. Bell's accomplishments in this matter are truly superb, but it should be remembered that an elephant's brain is about the size of a football, and that Bell was habitually shooting at rock-throwing distances. The problem of hitting the brain was negligible, but the problem of knowing where the brain was in that huge head was very considerable. Thus, we may consider that Bell's success was due primarily to anatomical knowledge rather than to masterful marksmanship.

While on the subject of Bell, it was remarked that he was frequently seen to take a goose on the wing with his hunting rifle. Now this is a good trick, but again one must evaluate the circumstances. An airborne goose at a target angle of 090 presents a nearly insurmountable problem for a rifleman, but if that goose is circling a pond and does not see the gunner, he will, for a few seconds on each circle, constitute a stationary target quite large and not very far away. I certainly do not wish to denigrate Bell's skill in any way, but the exploits upon which his mastery appear to be based do not add up to incredible marksmanship.

The story of Alvin York has been retold endlessly (by Theodore Roosevelt, among others), and it is a grand tale. As is well known, York earned the Medal of Honor by overwhelming an entire company of enemy machine gunners, single-handed, with his GI battle rifle on 8 October 1918 in the Argonne Forest in northeastern France. It is a great story, but when one analyzes it carefully, certain flaws appear. All honor to Sergeant York (who was promoted from corporal after his heroics), but here again we may not use him as an example of perfected rifle marksmanship.

Lt. Sam Woodfill, who also earned the Medal of Honor, and within days of Sergeant York's exploit, may be a better example of the rifleman in war, but he did not achieve the publicity that Roosevelt conferred upon York. When his company was stopped by well-emplaced German machine-gun positions, Sam Woodfill, who was a highly trained professional enlisted man before his temporary promotion, went forward with his 03 and broke the enemy position by skillful use of ground, cover, and unfailing deadliness with his rifle. Here we have a combination of valor, skill-at-arms, and astonishing good fortune. His use of that 03 was absolutely splendid. How difficult the shooting problems were is impossible to determine now, but whatever the difficulty, Woodfill was up to it.

During the great hunting days of the 1920s and 1930s, the American novelist and adventurer Stewart Edward White stands out, partly because he was extraordinarily successful in the game fields, but more so because his talents were analyzed rather carefully by E.C.

Crossman, who was one of perhaps a half-dozen truly authoritative "gun writers" of the 20th century. White and Crossman were both Californians, and by the time White had established his reputation in Africa as a miraculously successful field rifleman, Crossman had the opportunity to invite him out to the old Burbank Rifle and Pistol Club range for a session. The results were fascinating. Crossman, who knew all about military and sporting rifle competition and had written books about it, discovered at once that White knew practically nothing about the theory of rifle shooting, but that he made up for this by a combination of superb inherent eye-hand coordination and an athletic body that appeared unaffected by any sort of stress or strain.

White could not get into what Crossman regarded as a satisfactory shooting position, and he knew nothing about the shooting sling. White did not shoot small groups, but he shot consistent groups. He could keep all of his shots in a four-inch ring at a hundred steps under all conditions of light, speed, and position. Calm or out-of-breath, lying down or standing up, in slow fire or in a hurry, White's shot always landed within two inches of his exact point of aim. This sort of thing will win no medals in competition, nor will it be extolled by the advertisers, but it will do what needs doing—and it will do it every time. I have the greatest respect for all the legendary heroes of marksmanship, but I think I must put down Steward Edward White as a "Certified Master of the Art."

When considering the objectives of a shooting program, I have settled upon the premise that the object of the practical rifleman is the achievement of *first-round hits, on appropriate targets, at unknown ranges, from improvised firing positions, against the clock.*

The first round must hit. There is such a thing as a "firestorm," occasionally applicable to infantry engagements. There is also formal competition, in which practically inhuman consistency, shot after shot, is required. But the rifle is a weapon, and the second shot rarely matters. Very seldom will your elk stand there and wait for you to hit him again. If you drop an enemy with your first round, his buddy just may stand there and look blank while you try again, but do not count on it. The rifleman must put his whole mind on that first shot and bend his entire concentration to that effort, to the exclusion of all distractions. Thus it is that shooting "strings" on paper targets, while challenging, is not a productive shooting exercise. We must do it frequently, for administrative reasons, but we should remember that only the first shot of the string is important.

The term "appropriate" target needs defining. Rifle cartridges come in varying powers, ranging in efficiency from squirrel to elephant. The appropriate target is the vital zone of the creature to be shot, whether it is a prairie dog, a mountain sheep, a lion, an enemy soldier, or a rapist caught in the act. The size of this vital zone obviously varies, and the hunter has more leeway with his elk than with his deer. In practice and training, therefore, it is essential to concentrate on a target area within which the cartridge under consideration may be absolutely counted on to terminate the action. This will depend, of course, upon the size of the target and, to some extent, the power of the cartridge. In hunting, we generally assume that a circle or oval that delineates the vitals of the animal pursued is in the forward section of its body cavity. In fighting, we attempt to center our adversary, unless we can only see part of him, in which case we center that part of him that we can see.

The ranges at which we fire in the field are generally unknown. This is not as significant as it may sound, because modern rifle cartridges describe trajectories that may be counted on to stay well within the vital zone of live targets out to a point beyond which the shooter is unlikely to be able to group his shots—always remembering that the field shot is always taken under conditions less stable than those of the target range. At what we may call normal ranges, the shooter rarely needs to adjust his aiming point for distance. This is not always true; circumstances may arise where an extremely long shot is advisable. Under these conditions, the shooter must hold high and attempt to drop his shot into the vital zone. This can be done sometimes in fighting, but the hunter who tries it in the game fields should write himself a longhand apology, in triplicate, explaining why it was necessary for him to do it. Firing positions on the target range are specified. In the field they are improvised, and the target range is proper preparation for the field. Thus the shooter should be familiar with all standard firing positions, and a good many that are not, depending upon immediate surroundings. In the field, the shooter will be confronted with the problem of position selection, and he must be ready to meet it. In training I have always attempted to inculcate a critical evaluation of firing position. The principle is to shoot from the steadiest position available. A firing rest is always a good idea, and trees, fence posts, and rock outcroppings are more common than you might expect. Such are not to be counted on, however, and the shooter must cultivate the habit of instant position selection, adapted to terrain and time.

The shot must always be delivered against the clock—in the shortest possible time. Only rarely will your target be totally unaware of your presence and allow you time to deliberate. If such an opportunity is afforded you, be grateful; but do not expect it. Even when the target appears to be unaware, there is always the probability that it will move in a matter of seconds. Therefore, all field shooting practice should be carried out under conditions of restrictive time—not restricted by the clock, but restricted by the talent of the shooter.

I must conclude that I do not really know how to define a good shot. We encounter the same problem when we ask what constitutes a good pilot. Rifle marksmanship is a generalized talent covering many different attributes. When a person has shot the rifle over a long period, under a variety of circumstances, and has always been satisfied with his performance, I suppose he can qualify himself as a good shot. The combination of manual dexterity, nerve control, theoretical competence, and attitude constitutes the total effort. You cannot learn those things from a book, but you can acquire a sound basis upon which to build.

3
THE INSTRUMENT

This book is about shooting, not about rifles, but a few comments on the subject of the instrument to be used may be useful as basic information. The principles of rifle shooting apply to almost any sort of weapon that may be called a rifle, but for good or ill, rifles do tend to sort themselves into categories. In this book we will concern ourselves only with what may be called "serious" rifles—those intended for general service, rather than specialized missions.

Specialized rifle shooting is interesting, as in the case of formal target shooting, and it may be an entertaining sport, but overspecialization diminishes the virtue of the queen of weapons, which remains the general-purpose rifle.

As we enter the 21st century we find that rifle marksmanship has been largely lost in the military establishments of the world. The notion that technology can supplant incompetence is upon us in all sorts of endeavors, including that of shooting. The chancelleries announce that what is needed is a personal arm that does not depend upon the skill of the user but will accomplish a certain sort of mission no matter in whose hands it is placed. This may be the wave of the future, but it does not concern us here. Therefore, when we speak of a general-purpose rifle, we refer to an instrument that will do a great many different jobs equally well and that will reward skillful handling and the dedication that makes that possible.

The general-purpose rifle will do equally well for all but specialized hunting, as well as for fighting; thus it must be powerful enough to kill any living target of reasonable size. If you insist upon a definition of "reasonable size," let us introduce an arbitrary target mass figure of about 1,000 pounds (approximately 400 kilograms). If this proposition is accepted, the miniature calibers such as the 223 will be eliminated. The standard 30-caliber military cartridges in use through most of the 20th century constitute a starting point in cartridge selection. The classic 30-06 of the United States will do anything that a rifle may be called upon to do, which includes the taking of all forms of live targets, from prairie dogs to Alaskan moose, and it is superbly suitable for fighting. It is not wisely employed against buffalo, rhinoceros, or elephant, which at this time may be considered specialized targets.

The rifle should be a "repeater," permitting successive shots to be taken without reloading. It is most commonly found in what may be called "bolt-action" designs, which require the piece to be operated manually in some fashion between shots. A number of good self-loading actions are available, but they generally suffer from undesirable complexity and bulk, and they offer little in the way of increased rapidity of fire in the hands of a skillful marksman.

The most popular rifles today are fitted with optical ("telescopic") sights that enable the shooter to see his target more clearly, but do not help him to hold steadily or squeeze precisely. No sighting system can make a rifle more accurate than any other, but some are more convenient for the user. The magnification afforded by the telescope sight is not its most significant feature, and very good work can be done with telescope sights that offer no magnification at all. However, magnification of from two to four diameters seems to offer a bit

The forward mount of the Scoutscope permits strip loading in conjunction with a Mauser-type bolt action.

of additional edge without diminishing anything serious in the way of field of view or speed of use. It should be noted that the telescope sight may be a very quick system, but that excessive magnification diminishes this feature.

The red-dot electronic sight shows promise but is yet to be proven. This is also true of the laser sight and the various night vision sights currently found in military service. All of these technically advanced systems are expensive, awkward to maintain and adjust, and require self-contained batteries to be operative. Whether they improve the hitting ability of the marksman appreciably, or even at all, remains to be seen.

It is important that the general-purpose rifle be handy. Excessive weight and length may be advantages on the target range or from the bench rest, but they detract from the utility of the piece in the field. Speaking very generally, a rifle that is longer than one meter (39 inches) tends to be cumbersome for anyone engaged in active athletics.

If you can't hold it there for 60 seconds without discomfort, your rifle is too heavy.

Regarding weight, there is a simple test anyone can do in the store, on the range, or in the field. The shooter should grasp the piece with his right hand in a firing grip and hold it out shoulder high, at arm's length, muzzle vertical for 60 seconds. If he finds this exercise painful or even difficult, his rifle is too heavy.

Of course, a shooter can go too far the other way. A six-pound 375 may be so uncomfortable to shoot that its owner will not practice with it enough to perfect his skills.

The butt stock of the rifle is rather better too short than too long. A stock that is too short may tend to bump the shooter in the nose upon firing and may bang him in the eye if his scope is mounted too far aft. A stock that is too long, on the other hand, will render the weapon unwieldy and slow to use.

Thus it is that the stocks on military rifles are quite short, because they must fit anyone in the army. Contrarily, the stocks on most sporting rifles are too long, since a long (wooden) stock can easily be shortened by sawing it off. Stocks made of synthetic materials are more complicated to shorten, and the purchaser is well advised to demand a short stock on purchase.

I grew up on the short stock of the 1903 Springfield, which was notorious in the old days for bloody noses and split lips. At 6'2", I was too long for the '03 (as well as for the Garand), but I learned quickly to avoid difficulties by keeping my thumb over on the right side of the stock when firing and opening the fingers of my shooting hand slightly to avoid scuffing my chin with my fingernails.

The greatest single asset of the personal rifle, to my mind, is that it be "friendly." This is a difficult quality to describe because it is essentially a subjective matter. Nonetheless, it is very important. Your rifle should be your intimate friend and favorite companion. If you do not enjoy playing with it, walking with it, riding with it—it is just not right for you. Clearly, discovering a rifle that is friendly for you is going to take some experience. In this matter it is wise to profit by the experience of others and not to waste your time and money learning the hard way.

One aspect of the "friendliness" of a rifle may indeed be measured objectively, and that is the height of the line of sight above the axis of the bore. The more nearly the line approaches the axis of the bore, the more pleasing the rifle will be to shoot. Friendliness can also be predicted by the height of the shooting hand when in the firing position. For maximum ease of use, the middle knuckle of the middle finger of the shooting hand, when in the firing position, should be no more than three inches below the line of sight.

The general-purpose rifle will be equipped with a shooting sling of one sort or another, and the best of these is the type now known as the "Ching Sling," with its distinctive three-point attachments. Critically important in mountain and plains hunting, the sling can be readily detached and slipped through the belt when hunting in cover or in restricted light.

Your ideal rifle should not be intimidating. Bear in mind that if you attempt to reduce recoil by means of a muzzle brake, you are going to increase blast, and blast is more intimidating for most people than recoil. I believe that too much is made of this matter of recoil. I have taught many people who were on the small and timid side to shoot a rifle well simply by insisting that they ignore recoil. Recoil is just not very important, except in the case of long strings of repeat shots as are sometimes encountered in formal target shooting.

The most important characteristic of any rifle is its trigger action. It is better to have an inaccurate rifle with a good trigger than the other way around. A good trigger has often been described as breaking like "a glass rod." By choice, there must be no apparent motion of the trigger as pressure is applied to it, unless it is of a two-staged military style, which is managed by taking up the slack first and then pressing through on the shooting release. Obviously, the trigger has to move for it to accomplish anything, but that movement must be tuned down to the point where it is imperceptible to the shooter. The pressure required for release of the firing mechanism is better light than heavy, though the actual poundage is not critical. For me, 50 ounces seems very comfortable, but I should not use myself for an example because my experience has been too great. For most people, 40 ounces may be a better figure from which to start—I have a Blaser M93 rifle in my armory that breaks at 25 ounces, this being made possible by the radical Blaser trigger, which uses no sear.

A really good trigger action will go further in making you a deadly field marksman than any other factor about your weapon.

4
GUN HANDLING

The proper management of the rifle is not just a matter of hitting what you shoot at; it is also the efficient management of the weapon at all times—before, during, and after the actual shooting. The three elements of successful field shooting are marksmanship, gun handling, and mind-set. All are necessary: the absence of any takes the shooter out of the game.

It is interesting to note that gun handling is almost never taught in traditional schools. Safety is (and properly so), but safety, while it is an element of gun handling, is not the entire subject. As a matter of fact, safety can be overemphasized, because the rifle, as a deadly weapon, cannot ever be safe and efficient at the same time. As a Russian translator once said, "Eez gon! Eez not safe!"

The four general rules of firearms safety are easy:

1. *All guns are always loaded.* An unloaded gun is useless, and no one should ever assume that any piece he may see or touch is not ready to fire. Would that we would never again hear the plaintive wail, "I didn't know it was loaded!" *Of course, it was loaded.* That is why it exists. Treat it so!

2. *Never let the muzzle cover anything that you are not willing to destroy.* When you point a weapon, you

may not always actually intend to destroy, but you must be emotionally willing to do so. The fact that the piece is not loaded does not alter this. See Rule 1.

3. *Keep your finger off the trigger until your sights are on the target.* Guns do not "go off" by themselves. Somebody fires them. The competent shooter keeps his finger straight and outside the trigger guard until he verifies his sight picture. Violation of Rule 3 is responsible for about 80 percent of firearms mishaps.

4. *Be sure of your target.* Never shoot at anything that you have not identified. Never shoot at a shadow or a sound or a silhouette or anything that you cannot see clearly. Also make sure of what is behind and beyond your target that a bullet may penetrate completely.

These are the four general rules of gun safety. They apply always: while you are on and off the range, at home, in transit, hunting, or fighting. In studying them, you will see that if they were always observed by all people at all times there could be no such thing as a "firearms accident." As to that, it may be proper to insist that there *is* no such thing as a firearms accident—only negligence.

But there is more to proper gun handling than just safety. The rifle is a finely crafted, precision instrument, which will serve marvelously for generations under the most rigorous and hazardous conditions, if it is well managed. It should be kept clean, polished, and free from rust, and its working parts should be greased to avoid corrosion before it is placed in "dead storage." Naturally, when taken out of such storage, it should be degreased carefully before use. Its springs should be stored relaxed, though this is not as vital as some think in well-made weapons.

In "live storage," where the piece is in condition for immediate use, it is well to keep its lenses covered against dust and its muzzle stopped with some light material, such as paper tissue, to obviate the intrusion of bugs and such. The experienced shooter always glances through the bore of his rifle before taking it on an outing, and if it has been out of use for some time, he will pass a dry cleaning patch through the bore as a final precaution.

If the rifle has been out of active service for a while, it is always a good idea to check the tightness of all stock screws and sight-mounting screws, which should not back off on their own, of course, but which sometimes do.

Regardless of what advertisers may say, it is unwise to dismount and remount a telescope sight unless you are prepared to reconfirm your zero at the shooting site. Both telescopes and telescope mounts are supposed to come back to zero when removed, but long experience has taught me to be doubtful about this.

Unless you are prepared for action en route, a rifle is properly transported in a case. A soft case may suffice if the piece is to ride in the trunk of your car, but if it is to be handled as luggage a hard case is essential. Hard cases come in all descriptions, from excellent to unsatisfactory, and it is advisable for the rifleman to give case selection serious thought. When I hand over my rifle to the care of the baggage handlers, I make a practice of removing the bolt and storing it apart from the rifle itself. When nervous travel attendants ask you if the weapon is "unloaded," just smile and nod. Going into details will only serve to confuse them.

Before actually taking the field, you must always reconfirm your zero. This is usually done at your base camp, and it naturally should be done from a stable position. Do not trust one round. Even good ammunition can throw a flier once in a while, and, moreover, the human element may not be entirely disregarded. A three-shot triangle should be printed to your satisfaction before you conclude the enterprise.

When handling the rifle on the range, it is a good practice to keep the action open, but

16

when moving from point to point this may not be satisfactory because it may allow foreign matter to enter the works.

Conditions of readiness for the rifle vary with circumstances, and there is room for disagreement here. Sometimes you will have no choice and must honor the requests or demands of your host. I recall during the Rhodesian War when we went out through the wire a huge sign in red letters read, "Make Ready." On the back of that sign, where we could read it as we came back into camp, was a similar injunction commanding, "Unload." I think it is always a good idea to follow the rules, if possible, but I confess to disobedience of that second command in that war. In irregular actions one just never knows.

Generally speaking, when you hunt from a car or a boat, or when hunting in mountains or the desert, the proper condition of readiness for your rifle is Condition 3—that is, with a full magazine and an empty chamber. Instant readiness is not a normal requirement in such situations. When using a vehicle for transport and leaving it to shoot, it is considered good manners to mount and dismount without rifle in hand and to have the piece handed to you by a companion. One can, of course, envision situations in which this will not apply.

When hunting in thick cover, the rifle is ordinarily carried in Condition 1—fully loaded, cocked and locked. Under these conditions it is best to hunt alone, but when this is not possible be sure to observe Rule 2—as well as Rule 3. In the pursuit of dangerous game today, your greatest source of hazard is your companion's rifle. The professional hunters and guides of the world are well aware of this, and the stress factor of their profession is distinctly greater than that of, say, a race driver or a policeman.

When actually hunting, carry a reserve supply of ammunition. In a combat situation, of course, you pack as much as you can get. It is nice to think that you can handle any

problem that comes up with a single perfectly directed round, but that is sometimes wishful thinking. And remember, if you get lost in the bush, you will need enough ammunition for signaling, once you and your friends have agreed upon the signals.

Carrying systems are, to a certain extent, a matter of taste, but there are principles to be observed. Naturally, you will want to be sure that you never allow the muzzle of your weapon to point at your companion, your horse, your motor vehicle, or your cook tent. On long hikes you will probably carry your rifle slung either over the right shoulder, muzzle up, in American fashion, or over your left shoulder, muzzle down, in African fashion. You will probably alternate these for reasons of comfort.

When topping out a rise you should be looped up in your shooting sling, though this is not necessary with either the CW (named after my friend Carlos Widmann; for more information on this, see Chapter 11) or the Ching Sling.

When anticipating immediate contact, your rifle should be held in standard ready, butt on the belt, muzzle at eye level, thumb on the safety, and finger straight outside the trigger guard. Under these conditions, be sure that your muzzle points where your eyes look. It is the trait of a duffer to look to the right when his rifle is pointing to the left.

A "bird shooter's carry," over the crook of the shooting arm, is favored by some, but its support-side counterpart, in the crook of the left arm, is somewhat suspect because it continually allows the muzzle to point in directions where the shooter is not looking. If you are lucky enough to be carrying a Scout rifle, you will find that its handiness allows it to be packed easily in the fist of the shooting hand—at least for moderate distances.

In no case can I condone the "shoulder arms" carry, muzzle either forward or back. This is quite common in Africa today—a carryover from Colonial times. It makes me very unhappy. The horizontal position of the tube allows it to swing round, covering almost every point in the compass, and while it is true that the weapon will not go off by itself, there is a morale element here that I, for one, have not been able to overcome.

Back in camp, there are amenities to be observed. The first is not to get separated from your weapon, unless a gun safe is available, as is sometimes the case in modern African hunting lodges. In my carefully considered opinion, you must not be caught out of reach of your rifle. I have known many bad things to result from losing track of your weapon, and not only in war. There is, for example, the matter of attending to one's natural functions. Your rifle goes with you. I do not fancy unloading it, but some people do. If your host insists, very well, but be sure that you have that reserve supply of ammunition in your pockets. To the overcivilized, these precautions may sound excessive, but I have lived a long and active life, and I am still alive because I have always been very, very careful. Let that be a word to the wise.

Keep your muzzle out of the dirt. In the prone position there is a distinct tendency to drop the muzzle when the butt is placed into the shoulder. If you fire with dirt in the muzzle, you may not wreck your gun, but then again you may. This is not good.

During breaks in the hunt, I prefer to hang my rifle by its sling strap over a projecting tree limb or other solid protrusion, if one is available, but I never like to get more than two steps away from the piece. If I must go somewhere else, the rifle goes with me.

With modern ammunition, it is not necessary to clean your rifle bore every time it has been used. Still, when there is a break in the routine at camp, I prefer to swab out the barrel, wipe off the lenses, and examine and replace the ammunition in the magazine. It may not be necessary, but it makes me feel

good. Of course, before you pack up and head for home, the bore should be given a sound but temporary scrubbing, to await further attention when you are back at base.

Put not thy faith in safety catches! Gadgets can fail and sometimes do. The mechanical safety devices incorporated into rifles vary from almost completely safe to essentially negligible. There are safety devices on certain current rifles that, with wear, will eventually drop the striker when taken from a "safe" to a "fire" condition. There are safety devices that can be simply forced by the application of heavy pressure to the trigger. There are safeties that lock the trigger, but permit the striker to be jolted off by a heavy jar. Utilize the safety by all means—it will make the half-educated happier—but do not trust it completely.

This problem has given rise in certain parts of the world to the custom of lowering the striker on a bolt-action rifle by easing the bolt down as the trigger is pressed and then making it ready by simply raising the bolt and lowering it again. This is not a good idea. Obviously, the sharp blow on the head of the striker will fire the piece inadvertently. Also, it may fire if the weapon is dropped heavily on its nose on a hard surface. Naturally, one should not treat one's rifle that way, but circumstances have been known to get slightly out of control.

Above all, avoid the tendency to try to adjust mechanically to stress. Consider the man who gets down from his truck and follows the blood trail in Condition 3 until he feels unsafe, whereupon he works the bolt and slides a live round into the chamber, placing the safety on. Then, as he continues, he suddenly smells the quarry, so he nervously pushes the safety off. Then, as his heart pounds and sweat bedews his brow, he hears the stomach rumble loud and clear just to his right front. So now he puts his finger inside the trigger guard. Then, suddenly, there is a crashing snort, and he whirls to his right, puts his foot in an ant bear hole, and shoots his tracker in the knee. Bad show!

To learn proper gun handling takes a certain amount of thought, and its principles must be practiced. If possible, go to a good rifle school—one that features field shooting. If not, "let your gun be your companion on all your walks," as Thomas Jefferson put it. Get used to the rifle. Live with it. Handle it, and practice with it, empty as well as live. It has long been my custom when getting ready for a hunt to sit in front of the televisor during an evening with the piece across my knees, safety on. Whenever a commercial appears with the letter "O" or a zero in it, I attempt to mount the piece as I snap the safety off and achieve a clean surprise break on the center of that O. If there are two Os, as in Coors, it is up to me to snap that bolt and hit one and then the other before the inscription disappears. I have been chided on this as violating Rule 2, but I respond by saying that I can get along very well without my televisor, but I need my rifle skill. (And so far I have not blown anything away.)

A skilled rifleman will program his reflexes so that he snaps the bolt every time the striker goes forward—whether or not he intends to take a second shot. If he trains himself in this, he will never be caught with an empty chamber.

There is a tendency on the part of the inexperienced to admire one's handiwork when one has achieved a nice squeeze. Avoid it. Work the bolt—then gloat!

This reflexive bolt stroke must always be vigorous. If you ease the bolt open, you may not obtain proper ejection and may wind up with a jam when you try to close the action. If you ease the bolt forward, you may not close and lock the action all the way, which will usually result in a misfire. Bolt work must be vigorous. Show it no mercy!

5
SIGHTING AND
AIMING

T he sighting system on a rifle enables the shooter to determine where his shot will land. This system may be either metallic, optical, or electronic, though today the optical or telescopic system is the most common. It is important to remember that the sighting system on a rifle has nothing at all to do with accuracy, which is the function of the consistency built into the launching system. The sighting system enables the shooter to see, but it does nothing about his ability to hold or squeeze. It has nothing to do with the precision or the consistency of his component equipment.

Metallic sights may be separated into open sights and aperture, or "peep," sights. Both systems employ a forward index, or front sight, and a rearward index, or rear sight. With the open sight, the shooter endeavors to place both front and rear sights so that when they are viewed properly they will define the trajectory of the projectile. With the open sight, the shooter must try to view three points at once: his rear sight, his front sight, and his target. This is not physically possible, due to the focusing capacity of the eye, but approximations can be achieved. Thus, the open sight is difficult to use well. It stratified marksmen back in the days before it became largely superseded. It took exceptionally good eyesight to use open sights well on small targets at any distance. This does not matter much on dangerous game, however, where the target is both large and close.

The aperture sight is easier to use and generally obtains more precise results, since the shooter need only concentrate on his front sight and his target, and once he is looking through the rear aperture he need not focus there at all. The most efficient aperture sight for field shooting is known as the "ghost ring" because its combination of a relatively large aperture and a relatively thin rim causes it to disappear when the piece is properly mounted for firing. If a ghost ring employs a rectangular front post, it can be quite precise. A round front sight, or "bead," is difficult to align precisely for elevation.

Metallic sights have the advantages of being simple, reliable, and rigid. They require better eyesight and more practice than glass sights, but they are less prone to breakage and less susceptible to dust, dirt, mud, blood, and other foreign matter than telescopic sights.

With any sort of sighting system, the shooter must accustom himself to the idea that he looks along a straight line, but the trajectory of his projectile is a curve, and he must therefore endeavor to bring the line of sight and the curve of the trajectory into such coincidence as is suitable for his needs. Generally speaking, the field shooter does not adjust his sights in the field, but rather sets them so that he need not consider the curve of the trajectory at practical ranges. At extreme ranges, should he wish to attempt them, he simply holds high and trusts to luck. There are those who claim that the overhold can be brought to a high degree of precision, but I have only seen this demonstrated at measured ranges. In field shooting, the exact range is not known unless the field has been surveyed in advance or measured with a range finder. In such cases, a precise hit on the first shot is more a matter of chance than skill. I have seen such shots successfully brought off in the field, but while they are gratifying they are not something one brags about.

If a shooter is very sure of his trajectory, he may sometimes have occasion to *underhold*.

I remember doing this on my second grizzly bear, on which the shot was taken at about 100 paces, at which distance the expected trajectory of my cartridge (30-06/220) was adjusted some three inches high. The bear and I were coming up opposite sides of a shallow rise. I had expected to see him on the far side so I was already looped up; however, he was coming right toward me, and we saw each other simultaneously as we topped out. He stood erect to see better as I slid forward into prone position, there being no intervening vegetation. I put the reticle exactly in the center of his chest, and then, as I took up the slack in the two-stage military trigger, I lowered the aiming point a hand's breadth. I distinctly remember doing this, for I wrote it down in my journal that evening. (I have never had an occasion to do anything like that since.)

The combat shooter and the hunter have slightly different problems in aiming. In a fight you shoot for the center of mass or the center of what you can see of your adversary. He will rarely be standing erect and stationary, as he does in the combat simulators, so you will normally place your sights dead center and squeeze carefully. If he happens to be a long way off, stationary and standing erect, you may have the chance to do a bit of range compensation. If you have set a 200-meter zero and your target is 300 meters out, your best method is to place your front sight exactly on his shoulder line. If he is way out you may place your elevation index on the top of his head. These holds are not geometrically correct, but they will do as guides.

The only occasion of this kind in my experience took place at the Chirundu Bridge across the Zambezi River during the Rhodesian War. I was undercover on the south bank, and a sentry was walking post at the bridgehead on the north. I had an excellent rifle, a BRNO .30-06 mounted with a Zeiss telescope, and I was in a position to shoot from a field rest. I planned to hold about a foot over the man's head, but our security officer forbade me to shoot. He said that it might "cause an incident." It seemed to me that it certainly would, but it was his war, not mine, and I passed up the shot.

The major difference between the hunter's problem and that of the soldier is the fact that the hunter's target is normally a quadruped, and a quadruped offers a horizontal silhouette. The hunter must be more rigorously disciplined in his marksmanship than the soldier, because he owes his target a quick, painless death, whereas the soldier really does not care what happens to his adversary. (There is a theory that it is better to wound an enemy soldier than to kill him, because that will place a logistical burden upon the other side. It only does this, however, in static warfare, and I have never held it to be an important consideration.)

A major marksmanship problem for the hunter is knowing where to place his shot on an animal that may be of considerable size. On an elephant, for example, there is no problem in hitting the beast, but there is a very considerable problem in hitting him in the brain, which is about the size of a football and located somewhere within that massive Styrofoam skull. It has been said that hitting an elephant in the brain is rather like hitting a Volkswagen in the carburetor. You know it is there, but under varying conditions of range and movement the question of exactly where may be daunting. The renowned Karamojo Bell killed his hundreds of elephants with small-caliber, penetrative rifles, but he made a study of elephant anatomy and knew far better than most exactly what he was shooting at.

A common weakness in the novice hunter is his tendency to shoot at the whole beast without concentrating on the vital zone, which lies well forward in the torso. Four-footed grass-eaters are very frequently taken broadside, because they have a fatal tendency to stop and look back when they think they have outdistanced their pursuers. With an inexperienced field shot, this often results in placing the shot way too far back, with attendant unpleasant results. As a rule, one should take a broadside beast on the vertical line of his foreleg about one-third of the way up from the bottom of his torso, but a game animal is not a two-dimensional paper representation and must always be considered as a three-dimensional solid object whose vitals lie somewhere forward in his body cavity.

A heart shot is always fatal on a game animal (and usually so on a man), but it is not usually a stopper. Consciousness and mobility continue until the blood supply fails to reach the brain, and this may take some time. On a dangerous animal, this may be time enough for the beast to reach the shooter and return his attentions. If the rifle is of proper power for the task at hand, the shot should be placed in such a way as to impact the forward bone structure as strongly as possible. A shot that breaks into the shoulder joints, preferably on both sides, normally produces a quick stop.

The neck shot is advocated by many experienced hunters, and, of course, if the cervical portion of the spinal cord is severed, the target is stopped in his tracks. There is a lot of room in the neck, however, that is not inclusive of the spinal cord. When viewed from the side, the spine ordinarily enters the neck just behind the skull and then proceeds to drop quite low to the point where it enters the body. This means that a shot in the exact center of the trapezoid formed by the neck as viewed from the side will frequently break the neck. Not always, however. I once shot a handsome kudu bull squarely through the neck, because that was the only portion of him I could see that was not obscured by shrubbery. It is not easy to put a shot clear through the neck of a big beast like that, from one side to the other, without hitting anything vital, but I brought it off. My shot did not hit the spinal cord, nor the spine, nor the windpipe, nor any important blood vessels, and we chased that beast for almost eight hours.

In most four-footed grass-eaters there exists a "spinal flange" composed of vertical projections of the vertebrae above the spinal channel. At long ranges there is a tendency for the hunter to try to "help" his rifle by shooting a little high. If, in so doing, his bullet strikes one of the projections of that spinal flange, the beast will go down in its tracks, usually accompanied by a loud crack as the bullet hits bone. That crack and that instant drop are danger signs. In many cases, the target has not been injured in any serious sense and will be up and gone the moment it gathers its wits about it.

A mortally hit beast is often capable of running from 50 to 200 meters before it drops. The shooter should not let this distress him. If he is a good shot and he knows where his reticle was at the moment the striker went forward, he knows he has achieved his objective. If the range to the target was 100 meters or more, the *Kugelschlag* will come back loud and clear to corroborate his estimate.

When the target angle on a four-footed beast diverges radically from 90 degrees, the shooter should try for the far shoulder if the animal is running away or the near shoulder if the animal is coming toward him. In both cases, if the cartridge is powerful enough, the broken shoulder bones will be accompanied by decisive damage to the "boiler room."

From dead ahead, the shot is difficult, because the only satisfactory target is the spine beneath the chin and above the brisket. This spine may not be as broad as one would like, and if the beast is standing at a slight angle it may be difficult to locate. I have seen total success and total failure on buffalo with shots taken from dead ahead, with major-caliber rifles. I once got an icer, however, on a wildebeest, when the bullet missed the spine in the neck region but continued on into the torso and paralleled the spinal column about an inch to one side, for some 18 inches. I was shooting a 30-06/180, and there was plenty of power

available for a beast the size of a gnu—say, 450 pounds on the hoof.

At comfortable ranges the shooter should attempt to put his bullet one-third of the way up from the bottom line on his deer. As the range increases, he may wish to move his aiming point up until it is centerlined, top to bottom. If he attempts to hold over, however, he must remember that while he may be accurately compensating for bullet drop, he is also entering the area of bullet dispersion. The field shooter cannot shoot to an exact point, but rather to a shot pattern that increases in size as the range increases—and not proportionately. The "morning glory effect"—which, for practical purposes, states that the shooter of a high-velocity rifle (3,000 fps and higher) has little advantage over the shooter of a 2,500 fps rifle because at the distance when overhold becomes significant, range-probable error (which is dependent upon such things as wind, ammunition quality, and the shooter's stability) will become more significant than bullet drop—establishes that a one-inch group at 100 meters does *not* equate to a 10-inch group at 1,000 meters. If the shooter moves his horizontal sighting reticle up to the backline of his target, he is running the risk of placing one-half of his shots in the air, no matter how well he holds. I have seen this happen all too frequently in the field—and with some very good shots.

One is almost never justified in taking a shot from dead astern. This is not only impolite, but tends to wreck the carcass, and it does not bring the game down. There are exceptions, of course, especially those dealing with an animal already hard hit that is about to make cover. Naturally, the neck shot is available from dead astern, and I have seen it brought off twice in the field, but in both cases the hunter was an outstanding marksman.

I think perhaps the dryland hippo poses the most perplexing target. It is huge and uniformly black, but the problem is not hitting it; the problem is *where* to hit it. No matter how powerful your rifle is, that little bullet it fires has got to reach the right spot—and where is that?

It is clear the hunter's problems are different from those of the soldier. It would be a mistake to say that hunters are generally better shots than soldiers, because a great many people take the field after game animals who have not even partially trained themselves in marksmanship. However, it is safe to say that the sport rifleman is likely to be a better shot than a soldier and also a better shot than the one-box-a-year deer hunter, but as the revered Townsend Whelen put it, a man's skill in the field is fully as much a matter of his anatomical knowledge as of his marksmanship. *Where* to aim is fully as important as *how* to aim.

6
TRAJECTORY

In the days of my youth, basic physics was a subject required in high school, along with chemistry, biology, American government, and other arcane stuff. Today, it appears that such things are no longer offered, possibly because we cannot find anybody to teach them. The result is that a number of things I used to think were the common knowledge of voting adults do not seem to be so at all.

For example, take trajectory, which has to do with the path of a moving projectile, in air, if we are speaking of rifles. Not long ago I was astonished to discover a police firearms instructor of 18 years' experience who knew nothing whatever about trajectory and proceeded to teach pure error to his students when his department took up the study of the rifle. I suppose I should not be surprised at this, but still I am, and because this book is concerned largely with fundamentals, it seems a good idea to point out a few things about the path of a rifle bullet in the air.

If we postulate a bullet fired "horizontally," or more exactly on a path tangent to the earth's surface on discharge, it is acted upon by gravity, in a direction at right angles to its initial movement, the instant it leaves the muzzle. This is independent of its velocity. No matter how fast a projectile travels toward its target, it commences dropping the instant it starts on its way—unless, of course, it is not fired horizontally but at a slight upward angle, and this is, in effect, what we attempt.

The line of sight established by the sighting system may be considered to be straight—*pace* Einstein. When properly adjusted, the line of sight is *not* parallel to the axis of the bore. Moreover, the line of sight is not coincident with the bore, but rather slightly above it. Thus, when the projectile leaves the muzzle in its path toward the target, it rises slightly (when properly adjusted) until at a point some little distance out in front of the piece it crosses that sight line and continues upward at a slight angle. The point where it crosses may be termed the "initial intersection," and with projectiles starting in the 2,700 to 2,900 feet-per-second (fps) range, this initial intersection is located some 25 meters in front of the muzzle.

After passing the "double I," the bullet continues to rise, though acted upon by gravity, until gravitational pull acts upon it sufficiently to prevent any further upward departure from the line of sight. This point, which is often called "midrange trajectory," does not actually occur at midrange, but somewhat farther out than halfway, because while the bullet is moving through the air it is being acted upon not only by gravity but also by atmospheric drag, which, or course, slows it down. I prefer to use the mathematical term "maximum ordinate" (MO), rather than midrange trajectory.

Beyond the MO, still slowing down and still being pulled downward by gravity, the bullet continues upon its asymmetrical curve until it again crosses the line of sight. This second intersection is generally referred to as "zero," and it can be adjusted to any practical distance from the muzzle desired by the shooter.

Beyond zero the trajectory continues to turn downward with increasing rapidity, and this drop is more rapid than many shooters realize. At the point where the drop beyond zero equals the maximum ordinate, the combination has reached what we may call its "working range." If the MO and the drop beyond zero are adjusted to about half the anticipated vital zone of the target, the rifle may be used without any optical correction by the shooter. If zero is set for 200 meters, the working range of the combination will usually work out to about 230 meters, beyond which distance the shooter must hold his aiming point above what he intends to be his point of impact.

We note that *average* velocity (not *initial* velocity) between muzzle and target will affect the curve of the trajectory, but not nearly as much as many shooters (and most advertisers) would have us believe. A 30-06/180 zeroed to strike exactly on point of aim at 200 meters will drop seven to nine inches at 300 meters, depending upon its ballistic coefficient. The experienced rifleman, after having secured his precise 200-meter zero, will always check his 300-meter drop so that in the unlikely event that he may have to take a shot on a living target at that distance, he will know how to compensate optically for the curve of his trajectory.

In training, we first obtain a 200-meter zero, and then we move to a silhouette target at 300 meters, where, if the shooter holds his horizontal crosswire exactly on the shoulder line, he should drop his group pretty much into the area of the wishbone. If he attempts a shot at 400 meters (which he should not, except under unusual conditions), he can start by placing his horizontal wire exactly on the top of the head of the target, which should place his group center about in the solar plexus.

Initial velocity has less effect on the trajectory curve than is generally assumed because of the morning glory effect (discussed in more detail in the previous chapter).

High average velocity, with accompanying flat trajectory, is desirable, but no trajectory can ever be flat enough to compensate for bad marksmanship. The elements of trajectory are average velocity throughout bullet travel, bullet mass, and bullet configuration. Any projectile tends to hold its velocity in proportion to the square of its mass, something which I never understood until I began shooting projectiles much larger than those of sporting rifles. For example, I first assumed that the old 37mm antitank gun would shoot about like a 270, since its initial velocity was supposed to be the same. To my amazement that little 37 shot flat "way out past Fort Mudge" with minimal initial elevation. That was because its projectile weighed 2.5 pounds, rather than 130 grains. (There are 7,000 grains in a pound.) The nifty 88mm gun of the Germans in World War II shot flatter than a body could believe, to the amazement of those who encountered it.

All of the foregoing is well covered in elementary physics, a course that a good many rifle shooters never seem to have encountered.

There is a widespread belief that one should hold high when shooting uphill and low when shooting downhill. This is a myth. Gravity acts on the projectile in flight as long as it is in motion, and it will act in the same way regardless of the angle of departure of the missile. This angle is usually much less than we think—seldom more than 10 degrees. Even where the angle is quite steep, the time of flight to the target will not change appreciably under field conditions, and time of flight is what determines bullet drop.

If a bullet is fired straight up (a technically difficult feat), it will gain altitude until the combined forces of aerodynamic drag and gravity bring it to a stop. It will then come back down butt first, but because of the effects of wind drag, it will not return to earth at the same velocity with which it started. It will, however, retain most of its spin and land in the sand point-up, hissing in sinister fashion. The rotational speed of a conventional rifle bullet is very high, something in the neighborhood of 3,000 revolutions *per second*, depending upon the particular load and cartridge. Its travel through the air reduces this spin velocity very slightly, which is largely retained throughout the bullet's flight. The spinning of the projectile by the rifling is resisted by inertia very considerably, and this is why a smooth-bore weapon kicks so much less than a rifled arm of similar initial ballistics. A 1,000-grain round lead ball fired from a smooth-bore elephant gun to an initial velocity of more than 2,400 fps produces recoil that is almost gentle in comparison with that of a 600 Nitro Express rifle. It is interesting to note that this almost instantaneous spin applied to the projectile by the rifling produces a reactive force that is not distributed centrifugally, as one might suppose, but rather rearward. That is one reason why a modern smooth-bore tank gun does not require a muzzle brake.

The foregoing points are of only academic interest to the practical rifleman, the trajectory of whose rifle will normally be so close to the line of his sighting system that he will not be able to hold closely enough to appreciate it under field conditions.

29

7

THE FIRING POSITIONS

The shooter's body is the gun mount. It not only stabilizes the rifle so that efficient sighting can be achieved, but it also affects trajectory initiation by moving slightly as the projectile moves from the chamber to the muzzle. Consequently, the shooter's firing position should be as solid and stable as he can make it. The subject of firing position has been studied for a couple of centuries, and much has been learned about it. Oddly enough, this has not resulted in total uniformity throughout the world. Partly, this is because differing positions seem to work pretty well in proper hands, and partly because formal competition has made several sorts of firing stances mandatory.

Target shooting is a means to an end, and it is a good means, because it encourages large numbers of competing sportsmen to master elementary techniques. It should not, however, be regarded as an end in itself: the goal of the expert rifleman is a perfectly placed shot, placed by whatever system is most appropriate to the circumstances. The formal shooting positions are taught in the various military schools of the world and are called for in both military and civilian competition. They work, but it should be kept in mind that shooting in the field is the reason for rifle skill, and in the field one is not bound by regulations. Once the aspiring marksman has learned what may be called the standard positions, he should then cultivate the position to the best of his ability and fit his body to the terrain and the time limits pertaining.

The basic principle of the field marksman can be stated thus:

1. *If you can get closer, get closer.*
2. *If you can get steadier, get steadier.*

I was once chastised by a young lady I had taught to shoot when she returned from Botswana. "Jeff, you said to get closer. I tried, but the sable ran away." I suppose we should qualify the idea here by saying, "Get as close as you can, but no closer." Contrarily, of course, no sportsman ever takes a long shot just because he thinks he can. There is entirely too much nonsense appearing in print about long shots. A large portion of it is prevarication, and that which is not encourages bad behavior. When you start bragging about your long shot, you lose your audience immediately.

The firing position, of course, is the other side of this equation. It is up to the shooter to select the steadiest position he can achieve. Despite the fact that you must never take a field shot from offhand unless you have no other choice, I have seen far too many cases in which riflemen stood erect when they might have sat down, or squatted, or stretched out flat, or even used a bipod, or shot over a log rest. For a shooter to bring off a successful shot from an unnecessarily unstable position is no credit to him. On the contrary, it diminishes him in the opinion of any knowledgeable critic.

We will start by discussing the various standard positions, but we will always remember that there is nothing wrong with modifying a standard position if stability can be thereby increased. Modified field positions used to be called "jackass positions" in the old military service—a faintly derogatory term—but as we go along it will be apparent that all sorts of modifications may be improvised and will be by the master marksman.

PRONE POSITION

Prone is the most stable of the standard positions, and a good shot can hit about as well from prone as he can from a bench rest. Its primary advantage is precision, but it has several disadvantages. For the most part it calls for flat ground, because it does not offer much latitude for elevation adjustment. Second, it calls for a reasonably accommodating surface, because it does not work well in a swamp, a snowbank, or even in deep mud. Third, it takes a little time to get into, though this drawback can be lessened considerably with practice. Fourth, it radically limits visibility. Intervening grass, shrubbery, or uneven ground can render it useless.

The utility of the prone position in the field varies according to which field is being considered. I have seen it used successfully on mountain sheep, mountain goat, pronghorn antelopes, coyotes, wolves, and wildebeest—and I even used it once on buffalo, though in this case it was sort of a jackass prone position since I was leaning forward against the steep side of a *donga* with elbows on the parapet. The prone position is favored in military situations where, regardless of other considerations, there is a strong tendency to get close to the ground when pieces of metal are flying about. The last time I visited Fort Benning the only position being taught was that most useful from shooting out of a hole, which might be called "parapet prone." Under these conditions, I believe that a fist rest is probably a better solution.

Prone remains the steadiest standard position. Though I have never heard of a deer being killed from a prone position, the position remains a basic part of a rifleman's repertoire.

There are two common versions of prone: American military and Olympic international. We will take them in that order.

In military prone, the torso is flat on the ground with the legs apart and heels down. Minor adjustments in elevation are obtained by moving the right elbow in and out, causing the muzzle to depress or elevate. No elevation changes are effected with the left hand or arm, which are locked into the piece by the loop sling.

Military prone from the front.

American Military

The shooter starts standing erect with his rifle at the standard ready position, butt on the belt, safety on, finger straight, muzzle on target. If he is using a military sling, the shooter slings up before starting into position. With the speed sling this is not necessary as the sling can be set on the way down.

When ready, the shooter drops to both knees and advances the butt of the rifle forward to be used as a shock absorber as he continues into firing position. He then slides forward, catching himself with the rifle butt, rolls into position with his left elbow directly beneath the piece, and mounts the butt into his shoulder as his right elbow hits the ground. This should put him on target, and with practice, he will learn to drop into prone without any need to adjust for deflection. If a deflection adjustment is

The military prone position.

A modification of the Hawkins position places the shooter closer to the ground than "jackass" prone but limits dispersion in elevation.

The Hawkins position, using the left hand as a pistol grip, is very useful from a horizontal rest.

A modified Hawkins position using a horizontal rest.

The Hawkins position was developed by the Marine Corps in Vietnam. Its essence is the use of the forward sling mounting as a sort of pistol grip. The left hand seizes the two straps of the sling, holding it straight down, and uses the edge of the hand as a field rest. This position is useful in flat terrain when shooting at a target at the same elevation as the shooter.

necessary, however, the shooter will rotate the axis of his spine right or left to the point that when the left elbow is directly under the piece, the weapon need not be pushed right or left to stay on target.

If the shooter finds that he is pointing too high, he will pull his supporting elbow slightly in toward his body, raising his shoulder and lowering the muzzle. If he is pointing too low, he will reverse this by repositioning his right elbow. In no case should he try to correct a deflection error by the use of his left hand, which is properly looped up, placed forward against the forward swivel and with the palm directly beneath the piece. The fingers are not used to correct alignment.

The rifle is resting on the left hand, which is held in proper position by the tension of the sling strap looped around the upper left arm. That sling loop must be kept as high up into the armpit as possible. If it is allowed to slide down toward the elbow, it will serve no purpose.

When the prone position is correct, the shooter can turn off all his muscles and the sights will not move on the target because of the support the bone provides. This is the way you check your prone position. If, when you relax, anything moves, your position needs adjustment.

In the classic military prone position the shooter's legs are spread apart some 30 degrees, with toes out and heels on the deck. For maximum stability, you want nothing flying in the breeze.

Olympic International

In Olympic international prone position, the spine is not aligned 45 degrees across the line of fire, but somewhat closer to the line of sight. The torso is rolled up higher off the ground than in military prone, and this is achieved by rotating it around its axis slightly to the left and bringing the right knee up to the belt line. The left toe is reversed and pointed to the right of the shooter. As before, the rifle is

supported by the sling strap, and the shooter checks his position by going limp.

I prefer the military prone position to the international prone, but probably because I am more used to it. In decades of teaching, I have discovered that preference is divided about evenly among students. The student should be allowed to use what is most comfortable for him and not forced to conform to a pattern.

SITTING POSITION

This one, in my opinion, is the most generally useful firing position for the hunter. It is less popular with the soldier partly because he wants to get as low as possible and partly because the sitting position is a little more difficult to get into and out of than some others.

It is extremely stable, or it can be once you understand it. In my target-shooting days, my scores from sitting were just about the same as those from prone. The sitting position is more flexible than prone, allowing considerably more variation in elevation. Sitting also gets your line of sight just enough higher off the ground to make a difference in some kinds of terrain.

There are three choices in the sitting position: open-legged, cross-legged, and cross-ankled. Most hunters use the open-legged. Most target shooters use the cross-ankled. The cross-legged position can be a very stable one when shooting exactly parallel to the ground, but it is a little more awkward to get into and out of than the others. Some of the finest field shooting I have ever seen has been brought off from the sitting position—on the part of people who understood it. If it is less encountered than might be expected in war, it still has its uses.

After the First Marines, under Col. Clifton B. Cates, ground up the Ichiki Battalion at the Tenaru River on Guadalcanal in 1942, a number of the surviving Japanese attempted to flee by swimming seaward through the shallow

In the Olympic prone position, the torso is rolled slightly to the left, and the right knee is brought forward, raising the torso off the deck.

The Olympic prone position.

Olympic prone from the front quarter.

Olympic prone position from right forward view.

The cross-legged sitting position is quite steady, but it is useful only from level ground, offering almost no latitude in angle of elevation. Because the left elbow is supported on the left knee, the loop sling is always preferred.

The crossed-ankled sitting position is most commonly seen in formal target shooting. It is very steady, but, as with the crossed-legged position, it affords little latitude in angle of departure.

surf beyond the sandbar. The Marines who had the task of accounting for them found that the sand sloped down to water's edge in such a way that the prone position was unsuitable. They looped up and hit sitting, using the '03 rifle (this was just before we adopted the Ml Garand). From the open-legged sitting position, solidly looped up, they were hitting heads out there in the water with almost every single shot. An eyewitness told me that the gunnery sergeant with that detail was meticulous in making sure that every rifleman kept his left elbow directly under the piece.

I should point out that the versatility of the open-legged sitting position was very apparent to me on the event of my first bighorn hunt. I was directly above him and shooting downward at such a steep angle that my left hand on the fore-end was placed directly on the instep of my left foot. It was not a long shot, but the firing position was as stable as the mountain I sat on, and the kill was instantaneous.

In acquiring the sitting position, the first thing to do is to loop up, because both elbows are going to be supported. With the military sling you loop up before you go down. With the speed sling you loop as you go down.

The body is half-turned to the right of the line of sight, as with the prone position. When ready, you simply sit straight down, catching yourself with the palm of your right hand, if necessary, and placing your posterior on the deck. In the good old days we used to start on the range standing where we were going to sit with ankles crossed and right hand out behind the starboard buttock ready to catch. Since then I have discovered that one does not start shooting in the field in that fashion, since one is nearly always running into position with no time for artificial preparation. In practicing acquisition of firing position, the shooter should normally start three or four paces to the rear of the spot from which he intends to shoot.

With the posterior on the ground, the

The open-legged sitting position is one of the most useful options. It is easy to acquire and offers great flexibility. Note that the spine is slanted well forward and both elbows are placed inside both knees.

The open-legged sitting position permits great variation in angle of departure, which is most useful in mountain hunting.

spine is inclined well forward so that the upper arms can rest inside the knees. As with all sling-supported positions, the body should be rotated to the point that, when the rifle is exactly on-line, the left elbow is directly beneath the piece. The right elbow is supported by moving the right foot in and out on the ground until it is comfortably supporting the shooting arm. It is important to lean well forward, and generations of gunnery sergeants have spent much time kneeling on the shoulders of trainees to ensure this.

As in prone, the sitting position is tested by going limp. If the sights move off the target, the position is not quite right and must be adjusted accordingly.

It is a common error to sit erect and place the points of the elbows on the points of the knees. This looks very genteel, but it is inefficient, as too many "ball joints" are left free to wobble. People come in different shapes, of course, but ideally the left upper arm

The open-legged sitting position also affords maximum elevation adjustment, which is useful when plunging fire is required.

should lie flat along the inside of the left shinbone, affording a solid, stable contact. From this position I took the longest shot I have heard of on a buffalo, which had been hit solidly twice with a 375 by my shooting partner and was just about to achieve dense cover. This was an emergency, and I do not recommend shooting at running buffalo at 175 paces. It appeared to be necessary, however, and it all turned out well, as the bull crashed violently on his nose at the impact of my 460.

The cross-legged sitting position can be extremely stable and is thus much favored by beginners, but it is both awkward and a bit slow. It is assumed by pulling both legs up tight against the thighs with the left shin uppermost. This dampens the flexibility of the thighs, which sometimes bothers the novice because the thighs are essentially resting on the ankles, which are resting on the ground. The trouble here is that very little flexibility is available in elevation. To shoot cross-legged, you sit on level ground and shoot at the target which is on your own level. This works on the range, of course, but in the field it is not convenient.

The cross-ankled position is also very comfortable on the range and for somewhat the same reasons, because it does not permit much up-and-down flexibility. In cross-ankled sitting, the shooter does not face as far to the right of his line of sight as with the others, but more on the order of 30 degrees. Sitting on the ground the shooter extends his legs forward toward the target, straightening the knees and placing the left ankle over the right. If he then leans well forward, he can place both elbows on the inner surfaces of both knees, which are relaxed and not held in tension as with the open-legged position. This is the version of sitting that is currently most popular with target shooters. The shooting sling is always used where possible. I have never known either the cross-legged or the cross-ankled sitting positions to be used in the field or in combat, but this does not mean that it has not been done.

In over half a century of hunting, I believe that I have taken about 50 percent of my shots for "blood" from the sitting position.

"RICE PADDY PRONE"

This position, sometimes inelegantly referred to as the "military squat," was never taught to me in my youth and is not currently used in target shooting. It can be quite useful, however, because it can be acquired almost instantaneously and left with a single bound. It differs from sitting in that the shooter does not sit on the ground, but rather squats on his haunches with both feet flat and both elbows resting on the insides of both knees. This position is well adapted to the modern speed slings—the CW and the Ching—because, with a little practice, the shooter can loop up in the air as he leaps from a dead run into the squat.

When you get used to this position, you will find that you can change direction radically

The military squat, or "rice paddy prone" position, is not as steady as conventional sitting, but it is much quicker to acquire and exit. Because the left elbow is in support, the loop sling is advisable.

In all supported positions, the left elbow is placed directly under the piece, and the left hand is relaxed.

The kneeling position is popular but relatively ineffective because it affords no support for the right elbow. The "rice paddy prone" position should be used in preference to kneeling when possible.

simply by bouncing. Also, you can drop into the squat from a run, fire a carefully controlled shot, and bounce out of it, taking hardly more time than you would from offhand, but with decisively superior stability. This is a great charge-stopping position, combining both speed and precision, but it should be practiced assiduously if it is to be used with a hard-kicking rifle suitable for dangerous game. The shooter must be prepared at the shot to take a short half-step to the rear with his right foot to avoid being rolled over backwards, with attendant embarrassment if a large and bellicose beast is closing the range at a run. Remember that in stopping a charge it is not sufficient simply to smack your animal—you must place your shot with extreme care or suffer the consequences.

KNEELING POSITION

This shooting platform was much favored by Theodore Roosevelt ("Roosevelt the Great"),

but it is necessary to understand that while TR was one the greatest men America ever produced, he was not much of a marksman. Among other things he could not see very well. This may be irrelevant, but for whatever reason, I have never favored the kneeling position. It was my poorest stage in target shooting, and I have never killed anything or anyone from it. It is, however, a standard training exercise and one with which the rifleman should be familiar.

Because, in kneeling, the left elbow is supported, the loop sling is always used when available.

To assume the kneeling position, simply face right and go straight down until your right knee hits the ground outward from the left thigh at about 45 degrees. The left elbow is placed forward of the left knee joint and supported thereon. Left hand, left elbow, left knee, and left foot should all be held in the same vertical plane.

The right elbow rides in the air, and herein is a problem, because while the kneeling position gives pretty good stability in the up and down directions, it offers nothing much from side to side. That right elbow should be kept at the same level as the right shoulder to avoid recoil punishment of the upper right arm.

The right toe should be turned under, affording a quick kickoff should that become necessary. This may turn out to be painful for some people, but to point the toe straight out to the left reduces the usefulness of the position somewhat. In international target circles it is customary to see a shooter stuffing a shot-loaded leather bag underneath his right instep. I suppose this would be useful where one always has properly trained servants in attendance.

STANDING POSITION

(There is some confusion between the terms "standing" and "offhand." *They are not the same*, and they serve different purposes, so we will discuss them separately.) The standing position is used in slow-fire only, because it is deliberate and does not permit proper bolt work.

To achieve it the shooter stands erect, profiling toward the target with his left elbow resting on his left hip and his spine slanting rearward from the hips. The sling is not used. From the left hip, the left forearm points vertically upward, with the left thumb placed under the trigger guard and the fingers of the left hand forming a sheaf supporting the floorplate. On rifles intended for this kind of shooting, there is often a projection on the toe of the buttstock, which, when hung under the armpit on the right side, relieves the muscles from the task of preventing the weapon rotating downward over its support positions. Likewise, on rifles intended for this kind of shooting, there is often a palm rest extending down from the magazine some five or six inches, which can then rest in the palm of the

In the standing position, which is always deliberate, the shooter supports his left elbow on his left hip, places his left thumb directly beneath the trigger guard, and his left fingers in a sheaf just forward of the magazine well. He allows his spine to slant rearward from the waist. Only rarely is a shooter well advised to use this position in the field. It is somewhat steadier than offhand, but it is slow. Intervening vegetation is about its only proper justification.

left hand with no need of finger support. With rifles using extended magazines of 20 rounds or more, the magazine itself may be used as a palm rest.

In target-shooting circles we sometimes see shooters who wear a very massive, heavily padded glove on the left hand and who, when assuming a standing position, will rotate the left hand to the right until the palm faces directly astern and then close the fist to allow the rifle to rest on the pad of the left glove.

Shooting competition using the standing position has a long tradition in Europe where it is sometimes termed "free rifle" shooting. It is the heart of the alpine *Schützenfest*. Although this sort of shooting hardly has any practical application, it is great fun, and it is arranged so that while you have to be a pretty good shot to look good, the best man does not necessarily win. The traditional range is 300 meters, usually set up across a V-shaped alpine valley. The rifles are long and heavy and equipped with set triggers. Optical sights are not allowed, and the rear aperture, referred to as a "diopter," is formed of a very large disk with a tiny pinhole in the middle. The target is a black bull's-eye one meter across, and a good shot can generally hit it, in the absence of excessive crosswinds. However, the target rings are very close together, moving from a very small 10 ring at the center out toward the edges. That means if you get all your shots in the black, it will still be largely a matter of luck what kind of a score you achieve. No one can hit that tiny 10 ring consistently from the standing position at 300 meters, but if from month to month you keep your group diameter down, you will wind up the season in good repute.

The thing I noticed at once in the Alps was that at each firing point there is a wooden pedestal located about elbow high. I assumed that this pedestal was to serve as a place to put your ammunition. Not so. This is where you place your beer stein. Competitive shooting is a fine, old tradition in the Alps, and one can see why.

Apart from sport shooting in the Alps, I do not see the standing position as practical. If one has time to shoot slow-fire, one has time to acquire a stable position. I have used the standing position but once in the field, and that happened when I peered over the top of a pile of driftwood. I was just able to make out a little tropical whitetail buck on the far bank of the Rio Ixcán. I could not use that pile of driftwood as a rest because I could not reach its crest, and I could not lower my sight line even a matter of inches without losing sight of the target, so I shot from a very authentic free-rifle position, and while the hit was not as perfectly placed as I might wish, it did the job, and we feasted the troops.

OFFHAND POSITION

Whereas the standing position is deliberate, the offhand is not. You may see a number of local contests in which the shooter is called upon to shoot slow-fire from offhand, but this is because nobody thought up the problem before making up the rules. The offhand position is quick. If the shooter takes more than three seconds to align his sights and achieve a compressed surprise break, he must practice hard until he can do it right.

The sling is not used from either the standing or offhand position. In my youth several coaches encouraged the use of what was called the "hasty sling." It never did anything for me, and it is geometrically unsound. If you are hunting thick country, in fog or at night, it is best to take the sling off your rifle and thread it through your waist belt. It may be useful for packing out your meat if you are successful, but it will do nothing for your shooting.

To take the offhand position correctly, face 90 degrees to the right of your line of sight, hold your head erect, and raise the rifle until the sights are aligned on the target at the level of your shooting eye. Unless you have a Kentucky rifle, or something of the sort, the butt will be its full depth above your shoulder. Next hold the rifle and the head properly and point at the sky with your right hand. Now bring your right hand down in an arc until you can place it in a firing grip, keeping your elbow high. There is your offhand position.

Always assume the offhand position quickly. If when you find a target in your sights you have a couple of seconds to spare, so much the better, but always practice as if that target was about to disappear.

Practically all brush hunting is done from offhand. It is customary, likewise, on dangerous game, though we must remember that dangerous game is not always initially encountered at rock-throwing distance. One

The standard offhand position.

man's experience must not be taken as definitive, but I can say that the last three buffalo I encountered were taken at 11, 15, and 9 paces, and my one and only lion at 11. (But then there was that escaping buff at 175. One never knows.)

Perhaps the very best practice for offhand shooting with the rifle is the flying clay bird going straight away. This exercise does not pretend to duplicate reality, because one does not hunt quail with a 30-06, but it is a wonderful conditioner because it matches sighting and trigger control against time in a way that is hard to duplicate. Obviously, there are not many places where you can shoot a rifle at flying clay birds, but such can be found—given enough time and determination. Along some coasts it is possible to shoot out to sea, against the side of a mountain canyon, or over an uninhabited desert or Arctic snowfield.

To engage in this exercise, the shooter stands right at the trap with his rifle in standard ready, butt on the hip, safety on, finger straight, and muzzle pointing right where

The proper offhand firing position from the front and side.

To achieve a classic offhand position when the shooter is under no time pressure, he profiles toward the target, holding his rifle with both hands extended downward and with his head held erect and turned toward the target.

He then raises the rifle, using only his left hand, until its sight line is aligned with his target.

Next, he points his right arm directly skyward, thus raising his shoulder until it is in line with the rifle butt.

He lowers his right hand and places it in a firing position, being careful to keep his head erect.

In the classic offhand position, the left elbow is held directly beneath the piece, the right elbow is kept as high as the right shoulder or a little higher, the head is erect, and the left hand is relaxed.

second to be sprung at the first shot. Any shooter who can powder his first bird, snap that bolt, and catch the second has reason to be proud of himself.

JACKASS POSITIONS

These are improvisations, and they are difficult to teach because the circumstances that make them advisable are not easy to prepare. We may, however, go down a list suggesting what we are after and let the aspiring marksman work these things out for himself on his field trips.

Jackass Prone

Jackass prone is taken when shooting over a rise. The elbows and chest are employed exactly as in normal prone, but the body slants down to the rear. This is very common in military circles when shooting out of a shell hole or a ruined trench or over the body of a disabled vehicle. In all such cases the fist rest may be practical, and if so it may be a little better than jackass prone.

Jackass Sitting

Jackass sitting is used when the shooter has something to sit on other than the ground, for example, a chair or log. In this position the elbows are often rested on top of the knees, but not point-to-point. Always shove the elbow forward of the knee joint so as to achieve a flat-to-flat, if possible. I took my best-ever pronghorn, at a distance too great to be sensible, from jackass sitting. I have also used this position on Scandinavian moose.

Jackass Kneeling

One may sometimes find oneself standing in the bottom of a gully that, because of the shape of things, does not permit jackass prone. In these circumstances it is often possible to advance the left foot well up the side of the

the shooter expects the bird to top out. When the trap is sprung, the shooter mounts his rifle as he takes off the safety, keeping both eyes wide open and pointing his rifle as if he were going to shoot without sights. As the bird approaches the top of its arc, the shooter shifts from support eye to shooting eye, and when he has the knack he will see that the bird is flying right in the center of his telescope field. At the top of its arc, the bird will be effectively stationary for a bit more than a second, during which time the shooter must manage a compressed surprise break. If, when the striker goes forward, those crosswires exactly quadrisect that flying clay target, the bullet will powder the bird.

This is not easy, nor should one expect a great deal of consistency. One bird out of ten is satisfying, two out of ten exhilarating, and three and above is unusual. To add to the exercise, it is wise to use two traps, the first to be sprung on signal from the shooter and the

The "jackass" prone position is useful when shooting out of a hole or depression. From the shoulders forward, it is exactly like normal prone, but the body is allowed to angle down behind cover.

The "jackass" sitting position using a seat improvised in the field. This is particularly useful in watch-and-wait situations.

slope, leaving the right foot approximately in the bottom. The shooter does not kneel, but places his left elbow just forward of his left knee, as he would in the kneeling position. This position has the same weaknesses that standard kneeling has, but somehow it feels steadier to me.

Jackass Termite

I seem to have got myself involved with termite mounds in Africa in more cases than I hear about in the hunting yarns. Termite mounds let the shooter get his head above

intervening bush in many cases, but they are steep-sided and do not afford good footing. I have twice had to fire with my left foot wedged between a sapling in the termite slope while my right foot just hung out there in space. In both of these instances, I was able to grab onto some small-caliber vertical vegetation, which helped somewhat, but I do not recommend this procedure enthusiastically. If possible, go to the top of the mound and shoot from a fist rest.

I repeat this principle for emphasis, since it is not to be ignored: *If you can get closer, get closer. If you can get steadier, get steadier.*

8

THE REST
POSITIONS

The purpose of shooting is hitting. Any system or technique that increases the prospect of hitting the target is good. Therefore, when shooting in the field, either in hunting or in a fight, the expert marksman will always use a rest when he can. For our purposes, a field rest may be defined as any sort of object, nonintegral to the rifle itself, that may be used to support its weight, thus relieving the shooter of that necessity.

Bear this principle in mind: *The rifle itself must not touch the rest*. This is because the rifle barrel vibrates as the bullet passes through it, and that vibration must be consistent. If it is inhibited by a hard surface bearing upon the weapon, barrel vibration will tend to throw the trajectory away from the object it is touching. Normally, the rest will be the hand of the shooter, and that is not a hard object but rather a resilient one. Thus, the marksman, when using a rest, always places his hand upon the support and places the rifle in his hand. When shooting over a log, a rock, or the hood of a car, it is the hand that rests upon the support and not the rifle.

The rest may be part of the shooter's gear. It is said that Elmer Keith was fond of using the crown of his 10-gallon hat placed upon the ground. Jack O'Connor favored his binocular case, and the buffalo hunters of the Great Plains frequently packed along a

The bench rest serves to eliminate human error, and thus it is not a test of marksmanship, but rather of equipment. Note that minute elevation changes can be effected by squeezing the fork of the left hand, which supports the toe of the butt.

pair of crossed sticks, which would enable them to get above the level of intervening grass. I fashioned such a pair of crossed sticks back in junior high school, and I still have them. They never proved practical for me because I did not like the extra load they posed in the field; in my early days I never hunted from a vehicle, but had to pack along any chosen accessories—sometimes all day long. I note that prefabricated rifle rests are currently being reintroduced commercially, but in my opinion, there are few places where they are worth the trouble. Such places would involve the combination of vehicular travel and high grass.

Natural rests are another matter. Cattle country abounds in fence posts, and thin forest usually affords a tree rest every few paces.

It must be kept in mind that the field rest supports the weapon only in elevation and not in deflection. When practicing with it the shooter soon discovers that his piece is very

stable up and down, but that his body, supporting the buttstock, can wobble from side to side. The lower the body is to the ground, the less this lateral instability is apparent. When using the rest from prone, in the manner of Keith and O'Connor, it is not evident at all; however, the higher the shooter raises his elbows off the ground, the more he may be troubled by lateral wobbling.

STANDING

When you are standing erect and using a rest, the feet should be placed as far apart as comfortable, and the torso should face the target directly, rather than turned to the right as in offhand shooting.

When using a vertical post rest, the palm of the left hand is placed upon the vertical post, and the rifle is placed in the fork of the left hand and the thumb. When shooting around the post to the left, the heel of the hand is placed upon the rest, and the rifle is supported similarly in the fork. It is important to make sure when shooting around the left side of a post that the weapon does not slip to the right and abut the post with consequent deflection error.

It is often expedient to seize the forward end of the sling strap, where it is locked to the rifle, in the left fist, and to use that fist as a base of support where it rests upon something solid. This is particularly useful in choppy ground or over the top of a slight rise or wall. In perfectly flat country, without intervening obstruction, the fist rest may be used from flat on the ground. It will be difficult for most people to get the butt into the shoulder when the rifle is this close to the ground, but it nearly always can be snugged into the muscles of the upper arm. This technique calls for rather unusual terrain, and although it should be understood, it is unlikely to be called for with any frequency.

The vertical post rest from the left side. Note that the rifle itself must not touch the support.

The vertical post rest from the right side. Note that the rifle must not be allowed to touch the rest.

The field vertical rest from the right side.

The field vertical rest from the left side.

SITTING

In the sitting position it is sometimes possible to use the post rest without supporting the elbows on the knees, but this technique should not be emphasized because the support of the knees on the elbows tends to stabilize the lateral motion of the torso.

In high grass or thin bush it is sometimes possible to seize a handful of vegetation in the left hand and pull up as the hand supports the rifle. I have used this technique twice in Africa—once on black wildebeest and once on buffalo—and while the range was not great in either case, the results were entirely to my satisfaction.

The integral bipod, either hooked onto the rifle after purchase or built into it by the manufacturer, is seen increasingly in the hunting field, and I have even noted it in the hands of domestic law enforcement organizations. It has its uses, though not always in actual shooting.

The bipod offers a very satisfactory means of verifying the zero right at the hunting camp, which often does not have a bench rest available. It affords a means of putting a rifle down on the ground without getting it dirty during breaks in the action. About the only shooting field use it is likely to have, however, is in ambush situations where the hunter sets himself up under cover and waits for his quarry to come to him. I have taken the Clifton integral bipod into the field on two occasions, but while it has definite convenience advantages, I have never yet killed anything from it.

I think the aftermarket bipod is probably an excellent feature of any well-equipped hunting camp, but should be used exclusively for zeroing because it is uncomfortable to carry afield when actually in pursuit. The integral bipod, however, which does not project from the weapon at all when folded and is invisible when not in use, is another matter. It does not lend itself well to wooden stocks, but in the age of synthetics it may be the coming thing.

The horizontal rest as used in the field.

When using a field horizontal rest, the rifle must be prevented from resting on anything hard. The left hand is used as support.

50

When a bipod is used in the field it is employed exactly like a bench rest. (Shown here is the Clifton retractable bipod on a Springfield pseudo Scout).

The assault bipod, shown here on the G3 rifle, is used much like a machine rest, with attendant advantages and disadvantages.

The assault bipod position can achieve surprisingly good hits at moderate ranges and is quite useful in run-and-jump situations.

The European hunter shoots mainly from the *Hochsitz*, and he shoots over a padded rest built into his stand. This is one reason why one never encounters the shooting sling in Europe. This type of shooting is always slow-fire, and it is difficult to arouse any interest in speed among people who have become used to it. I once hunted up in Rhodesia with a good friend from Germany who was an excellent shot slow-fire, but who became excessively rattled when called upon to shoot in a hurry. Certainly, most rifle shooting is slow-fire, but that does not mean speed will never be called for, and the expert marksman must be able to handle it.

Whenever he can, the shooter should shoot from a rest, but he should always remember that he is not thoroughly competent unless he can fire without one.

9

THE HAND AND
THE FINGER

The rifle is normally fired by pressure of the finger on the trigger. The firing hand is placed upon the buttstock of the rifle in such a way as to make this most convenient. There are two systems in common use, which we may call the forward grip and the rearward grip. Short stocks favor the forward grip, but because most "sporting" rifle stocks are too long (in my opinion), we may consider the two systems as equally viable.

With the forward grip the shooting hand is wrapped snugly around the "small of the stock" with the second finger up against the rear curve of the trigger guard, the thumb on the right side of the weapon where it most easily operates most safeties, and the trigger finger is placed on the trigger so that the groove between the first and second phalanges coincides exactly with the right edge of the trigger itself. Firing pressure is exerted by the movement of the trigger finger rearward, as the base of the first phalange, rather than the tip of the finger, makes the critical contact.

With the rearward grip, the palm of the firing hand is placed farther aft on the stock in such a way that only the tip of the finger touches the trigger, and the thumb is placed across the stock and rests on the left side.

I favor the forward grip for several reasons. It

keeps the thumb off the nose, it facilitates the operation of the safety, and it seems to provide me with a more positive finger-trigger contact. It is best adapted to the traditionally shaped sporting-rifle stock, whereas the rearward or fingertip grip is widely used on conventional combat rifles that feature a nearly vertical pistol grip. I have heard it said that the rearward grip facilitates the management of a bad trigger, such as is customarily found on combat rifles, but I am not sure that this is indeed the case.

A bad trigger (one that is both heavy and gritty) seriously hinders good marksmanship, but there are many such triggers in the world, and if you are stuck with one you must learn to make do. One way to achieve this is to pinch the trigger off by placing the thumb of the firing hand on the rear outside curve of the trigger guard and pressing thumb and forefinger together firmly until something happens.

I remember an episode from college days in which the "pinch off" system served me well. The rear of our fraternity house faced an open field in which a number of ground squirrels had set up operations. Standing on the second-deck sunporch I opined that I could take out those beasties, which are unsanitary nuisances, if I only had access to a good 22. One of the brothers immediately took me up on this, pointing out that he had his own 22 in his closet. Naturally, I had to accept the challenge, though I had indeed bitten off somewhat more than I probably could chew. The range was moderate, say on the order of 90 to 100 yards, but the target was very small since the only shots offered revealed just the head and neck as the creature peeked out of his hole. The challenger showed up shortly with his piece, which was a cheap, open-sighted, autoloading 22. Its trigger, when tested, was just awful, weighing six or seven pounds and crunching through almost a quarter inch of rearward travel before discharge. The project was most unpromising, but since I had been bragging

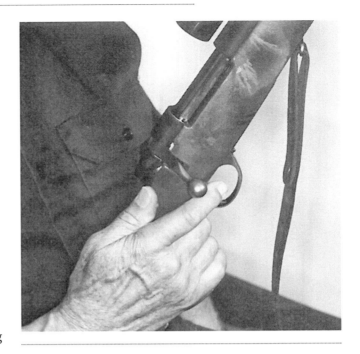

The forward grip.

In the rearward grip, the tip of the index finger actuates the trigger, and the second finger of the shooting hand does not touch the trigger guard. It is always advisable to keep the thumb of the shooting hand over on the right of the weapon where it facilitates both mechanical safety operation and quick seizure of the bolt handle.

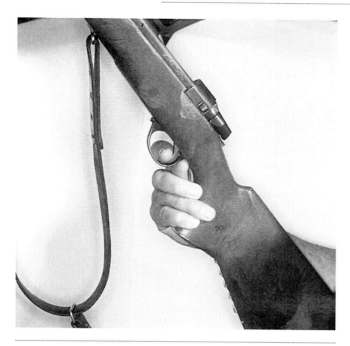

The pinch press.

about my marksmanship to the brothers, I was now called upon to prove it. (One learns with time never to boast about his shooting ability, but I was very young and had not yet learned that.) The customary wager, at that time and place, was dinner at one of the two good eating places readily accessible to the Stanford campus, Dinah's Shack and L'Omelette. If I missed the squirrel, I was committed to take both of us to dinner. If I hit it, the challenger would pay. I could do nothing about the sights except to pray that a six o'clock hold on a squirrel's head would do. I squirmed down into a prone position, using my fist on the railing as a rest. When the unlucky squirrel poked his head up, I pinched thumb against forefinger gradually but firmly—and pop she went. There was a small puff of dust at the target, but the beast was nowhere to be seen.

"Let's make it L'Omelette!" cried Jack, "and make it Thursday. I have a heavy date both Friday and Saturday." But, as it turned out, he paid. When we walked out to the burrow, we found the squirrel at the bottom of the hole, shot

squarely through the head. Luck was with me on the sights, but the "pinch-off" technique won the day. After all these years, I still look back on that incident with complete satisfaction.

There are three types of triggers in general use on today's rifles: the single-stage or shotgun trigger, the two-stage or military trigger, and the set trigger, either single set or double set. The so-called shotgun trigger is most common on sporting rifles, the two-stage on combat rifles, and the set trigger on European rifles.

When the single-stage trigger is properly set up, there is no apparent motion during its actuation. Clearly, there must be some, otherwise the trigger would not release the striker, but in a high-quality weapon, this motion is reduced until the shooter cannot detect it. When the sights are properly aligned, the shooter simply squeezes his trigger finger rearward until, at a moment not selected by himself, the piece fires. This is called the "open-end surprise break," and it is normal in rifle shooting from stabilized positions. When shooting hurriedly from the offhand position, the "compressed surprise break" of the pistol shooter is used. With this, the time in which pressure is applied is compressed into an interval selected by the shooter, which may be anything from a full second to practically instantaneous, but, of course, the trigger is never actually pulled or jerked. Ignition must always occur as a surprise to the shooter. (*Note:* This is not true of the "nudge," as used by target shooters in the standing position, but the nudge is difficult to learn and of little use to the field marksman.) With the two-stage trigger, the initial movement of the trigger must be achieved before the actual firing pressure is applied. This first movement of the trigger, which may be as much as a quarter of an inch in some cases, is lightly sprung and is referred to as "take-up." With a little practice the shooter will learn to differentiate absolutely between take-up and "creep," which is apparent movement of the trigger as it releases the striker. Take-up is perfectly okay; creep is not, and it should be eliminated by the careful attentions of a qualified gunsmith. This operation should properly be a function of the manufacturer, but sometimes it is not. In this distressing age of litigation, it is apparent that many manufacturers regard a really good trigger on their weapons as an invitation to a lawsuit, the notion being that if most triggers in common use are bad, an unenlightened shooter may be led to fire a good trigger inadvertently. This is why it is not easy to acquire a piece in current production with a really good trigger, unless one is prepared to pay the high price of good quality.

I prefer a two-stage trigger to a single stage, partly because I think it is mechanically more reliable but mainly because I grew up on the military trigger and find it more comfortable. Today, there is available a single-stage trigger with which the releasing action is totally imperceptible to the shooter and that does not require delicate machine tuning, either at the factory or aftermarket, because it does not employ any disengagement of the sear to release the striker. This is the trigger on the Blaser R93 rifle. In theory it is impervious to malfunction, but since it is quite new only time will prove it out.

The third common trigger system is the "set trigger," either double or single. This system has been around for more than a century, and it is found mainly on German and Austrian sporting rifles. Up until quite recently, it provided a rather heavy and spongy trigger action if the forward trigger was pressed without "setting" it. Setting was accomplished by pressing the rear trigger, at which time the forward trigger was placed at another mode, requiring only a few ounces to touch it off. Apparently the idea was to enable the shooter to use the coarse mode for snapshots, but permit him to set the piece up purposely for maximum slow-fire precision. More recently, however, Steyr-Mannlicher has been furnishing its new line of sporting rifles with a single-set trigger set simply by pressing it forward, with superb quality in both set and unset modes, and one I tested recently offered an extremely clean and apparently motionless release unset at 50 ounces. When set, it released at 11 ounces. This is a very considerable technical achievement, but I confess that an 11-ounce trigger release calls for more familiarization than I am inclined to render. The 50-ounce unset "glass rod" does just fine for me.

We should note at this point that the Voere system of electric ignition calls for no striker and no striker release whatever. The shooter simply informs the rifle when he wants it to shoot by closing a circuit with his trigger finger. The Voere rifles use a trigger at this time, probably because it is customary, but a simple, motionless, pressure-sensitive button would do as well. (Naturally electric ignition calls for batteries. In my experience, batteries are usually dead when you need them, but that is an old-fashioned view.) In all cases a good trigger should permit a smooth, effortless, surprise break, which is the essence of good marksmanship.

10

THE EYE

The eye of the rifleman serves him in two ways. First, it allows him to align his weapon correctly, and, second, it is his primary means of acquiring targets. The first is a matter of visual acuity, which is less important in the day of almost universal use of telescopic sights than it used to be. The second, which does not appear to be widely understood, has to do with the conditioning of what may be called the "control center" in the brain, which sorts out and analyzes the message delivered by the optic nerve.

It is a nice thing to have nice, sharp 20/20 vision. It is not absolutely necessary, however, to good marksmanship. For a man using the open metallic sights of the Kentucky rifle, excellent vision was a distinct advantage. With the aperture sight, it is less so. This is because when an open sight is used the shooter must attempt to focus on three different points at once: his target, his front sight, and his rear sight. This is not physiologically possible if the target lies any distance from the front sight. So what the shooter does is attempt to switch back and forth from one point to another, first on his rear sight, then on his front sight to achieve proper alignment, then on the target to select the desired point of impact, and then back to the front sight for firing. The eye is a marvelous instrument, and it can be trained to do this very quickly, but this does not alter the fact that open sights are not generally very efficient, except at the closest ranges.

The aperture sight is better, because the shooter may ignore the rear sight and concentrate only on the target and the front sight. As long as the shooter has a clear view of his front sight, it is not necessary for him to attempt to center that front sight in the light pattern afforded by the rear. It is surprising how many people do not understand this, but anyone who doubts it may prove it to himself by using alternative rear sights of varying diameters and observing the results. It is a common—and in my mind erroneous—view that the smaller the pinhole in a rear aperture sight, the better the shooting will be. I have experimented with scores of students in this connection, and I cannot establish it to be the case. (Of course, this is within reasonable limits. One can hardly expect good results with a rear aperture the size of his thumb.) The most useful front sight for a rifle is a sharply defined rectangular post, usually black but sometimes improved by the insertion of a vertical red stripe. The very common round front sight, or "bead," is less satisfactory for a number of reasons. The round bead offers a curved top rather than a straight line, which provides no precise index of elevation.

This does not matter on a charging lion at 10 paces, but that sort of target is not as common as it used to be (worse luck!). When properly adjusted, the aperture sight places the impact center exactly on the middle of the top of the post. When shooting with good aperture sights, the shooter places his front sight post on the target in such a way that his shot will land exactly on its top center. When the shooter holds off for range, he may wish to hold a tad low at distances short of his zero point and a tad high beyond, but when using modern cartridges and ammunition this may be something of an affectation, because the shooter is unlikely to be able to hold any closer than the departure of the trajectory from the

line of sight out to the working range of the combination. Beyond the working range, he may attempt to correct by holding a bit high until the distance involved renders his group size greater than his target.

It should be clear that when a rifleman is shooting at a black bull's-eye he should expect his group center to be located at the bottom of that bull's-eye unless he has set his sights otherwise.

The red center insert in the forward front post is used for accelerated acquisition, but it is no aid to accuracy. If a colored insert is used, it should be red or orange, not gold or white. Gold is difficult to discern against dry grass, a khaki shirt, or a tawny hide. White disappears against the sky, snow, or a white shirt. (I remember how apparent this was in the Aleutian campaign, where we discovered that the Canadian patrol airplanes, painted a dull white, were invisible against the perpetual mist of the Aleutians, except for their roundels.)

Shooting with a properly designed aperture sight or "ghost ring" can be very quick. The large aperture is easy to see through, and the thin outer rim vanishes because the eye is searching for a focus at the front sight and loses the rear ring once it has been seen through. The shooter ignores the rear aperture, glances over his front sight to make sure of his target, and then freezes back onto it for the shot. Experience has convinced me that what we now call a ghost ring, described early in the century by Karamojo Bell and E.C. Crossman, is the most satisfactory form of sight for a rifle intended to be used on dangerous game. By its very nature, dangerous game is most often taken at very short range. A beast is only dangerous if he can touch you, and the careful hunter will do everything he can to get as close as possible to his target, short of arm's length, in order to place his shot perfectly. For this purpose, the telescope sight is not only no help, but it may actually be a drawback for various reasons— not the least of which is fragility.

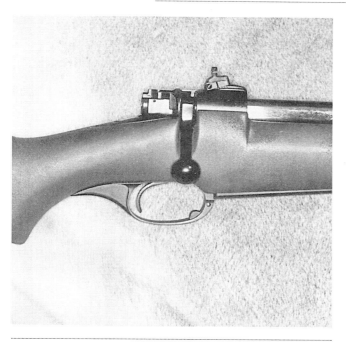

On a hard-kicking rifle, a trigger guard adapter diverts the blow.

Despite the foregoing, the telescope sight, or optical sight, is here to stay, certainly on hunting rifles and increasingly so on battle rifles. The principal advantage of the telescope sight is not its magnification, but its single focal plane. When seen in the glass, the aiming index or "reticle" is in the same focal plane as the target, obviating the necessity for the shooter to switch his focus back and forth from one point to another. Thus, the scope is the quickest form of sighting system—when used properly. When its technique is not understood, it may be quite slow.

A proper scope is mounted as low on the rifle as possible and well forward. Ideally, the rear lens of the telescope should be no farther to the rear than the rear curve of the trigger guard, but the designated eye relief of a good many telescopic sights is too short to permit this.

The closer the telescope is to the eye, the slower it will be to use and the more prone it will be to cause what has become known as "Kaibab eye," and the annoying custom of "getting lost in the scope." One reason that

many telescope sights are mounted too far astern is that when the customer in the hardware store picks up the piece he tends to point-in while standing erect, with his spine at right angles to his line of sight. However, when he rolls forward into any stabilized position—prone, sitting, or bench rest—his spine will be slanting forward, placing his head farther forward on the stock and bringing his eye closer to the scope. Thus, we see many well-made scopes featuring a rubber cushion ringing the rear lens of the telescope. If, when you fire a shot, the telescope belts you in the eye, you are doing something wrong. We can start out by assuming that you are mounting the telescope too far rearward on the weapon.

"Getting lost in the scope" is an aberration resulting from lack of proper technique. We see it all the time in the field, in this age when it is pretty hard to find a place that will teach you proper technique. The scene occurs when the rifleman spots a target, or a possible target, out some distance away on a far hillside. He immediately takes his eyes off the target and looks at the telescope, regardless of where it may be pointing at the time. Seeing nothing of his target, he then begins to search the countryside with the glass, without anything telling him where he should be pointing it except his memory of where the target was when he took his eyes off it. Besides simple ignorance, getting lost is aided by a telescope of too great magnification mounted too close to the eye. The correct technique in this case is to keep your eyes (both wide open) on your target while you mount the piece into your shoulder, as if you intend to fire without sights. When you have mounted your rifle properly and it is pointing as close to your selected target as you can make it, it is then time to glance through the glass with your shooting eye, and you will be rewarded by seeing your reticle placed exactly on what you selected when you mounted the piece.

The telescope sight is the most satisfactory

THE ART OF THE RIFLE

general-purpose system we have, but it does have certain drawbacks. It calls for very precise adjustment, and not every purchaser is qualified to carry this out. It gets dust, mud, or grease on the lenses. (Care must be taken to avoid this when in the field under hardship conditions.) It is almost useless in driving rain or sleet. Its internal adjustments break. The manufacturers will deny this at the top of their lungs, but the fact remains—they break. If the crosswires separate or the entire reticle begins to rotate, this is easily detected, but if the reticle just becomes loose in its mounting, you will not find this out until you deliver a perfect squeeze and come up with a clean miss.

Various manufacturers of telescope sights will insist that these things cannot happen with *their* brand, but that may be likened to claiming that one brand of tire will never go flat. When I used to teach rifle marksmanship regularly, I could count on one or two telescopes per class of sixteen breaking during the course of instruction, which involved between 300 and 400 rounds of ammunition.

Lastly, because any telescopic instrument is restricted by its field of view, it is sometimes possible to get so close that the shooter cannot tell what part of the animal he is viewing. This happened with me once on an exasperated lion, and it impressed me very much. If I had followed my own advice, I would not have chosen to bother that lion with my telescope mounted, but I simply assumed that I was not going to get that close. I do not know how long the delay was in which I shifted my concentration to my left eye, picked out a point to shoot at, and got back on. I do not suppose it was long, but it seemed so to me, and it must have seemed forever to Danie, my professional hunter.

Regardless of the type of sight used, the rifleman must devote his entire concentration to the selection of his intended point of impact. This may not be critical in a fight, because human antagonists are not very resistant to gunfire and are often disabled by a peripheral

hit from a serious cartridge. Besides, we do not shoot at human beings for sport, but only under desperate circumstances where considerations of sportsmanship do not apply. However, when shooting at a game animal, we must strive above all for a clean, painless kill, and we cannot get this by shooting generally at the body of the animal. The more powerful your cartridge in relation to the size of your target, the more likely you will be to secure a satisfactory stop, but no amount of power will make up for bad placement. The conscientious hunter will study the anatomy of his proposed game at length and in detail, remembering always that his target is a solid object with three dimensions and that he must place his hit well into the forward portion of the body cavity. (On buffalo this may not be enough. Therein lies the excitement of buffalo hunting.)

The second function of the rifleman's eye may be referred to as target acquisition. What we see is only the first half of this function. The second half is the translation of the optic signal into a message on which the brain can work. This so-called "hunter's eye" is achieved when the brain, by practice or possibly by instinct, makes the correct analysis of the optic signal and makes it quickly.

I ran into this on my first big-game hunt in the Canadian Rockies. We were traveling on horseback, and when we came up to a stream to let the horses drink, I would ask Miles, my Indian guide, if he had seen anything. Usually, he would point out that not only had he seen things, but that they could be seen from where we sat. "Across over there, up there on that hill, behind the reeds to our right." When he pointed these things out to me, I found that they were easily visible, since my eyes were every bit as good as his, but he knew what he was looking for and I did not. That is to say I knew in theory, but I did not know in practice.

Eric Hartmann, the German World War II fighter pilot considered by many to be the greatest of air-to-air fighters, was deemed by

In shooting from the offhand position, both eyes are kept open, if possible. This is easy if the shooter is right-eyed, but if his left eye is dominant, he may have to close it in order to give control to the right eye.

his comrades to possess almost supernatural eyesight. Medical analysis, however, recorded that his eyes, while very good, were simply high-average for the general run of fighter pilots. But Hartmann always seemed to find the other formation first. When he told his wingman where to look, the latter had no trouble in spotting adversaries, but Hartmann spotted them first and often so far away that he could count on his enemies not seeing him at all until it was too late.

A striking example of this matter of target analysis is the elephant in the African bush. The elephant is huge and nowise difficult to see, even for people with only marginal eyesight, but until you are used to it, you do not realize that you have been looking at an elephant until you have been looking at him for quite a long time. The optical signal was strong, but the control center in the brain was simply not prepared to analyze it.

For this reason, conventional target shooting and training is of almost no usefulness to the field rifleman. In my youth I was exposed to a number of "field reaction courses" in the military, most of which featured "pop-up" targets that were raised into view as the trainee trod the trail. These posed no problem whatever because the motion of their appearance was always enough to catch the eye. Much more sobering, on the other hand, were various courses of my own design in which the target was perfectly visible to the shooter on the trail for a matter of five seconds or so, at which point it vanished. These "pop-down" targets are decisively more useful in field marksmanship training—though they are somewhat hard on the morale of the student.

Of the many thousands of students I have taught, the majority have been right-handed and right-eyed. This is fortunate, partly because most rifles are built for the right shoulder, but secondly because while "cross-eyed" shooting does not pose a problem with the pistol, it does with the rifle. For a rifle shooter who is right-handed and left-eyed, the snapshot is difficult to achieve. The same would be true of a left-handed shooter who was right-eyed. In slow-fire these things do not matter very much, but as quickness becomes necessary, they do pose a dexterity problem.

Contrary to widespread belief, it is not overly difficult for a left-handed shooter to operate a right-handed bolt. Some of our most distinguished international competitors had just this problem and overcame it. Clearly, when a left-hander has to reach over his weapon to grab that bolt handle, he must take his left elbow off support, when shooting from prone or sitting position. I mentioned this to Gary Anderson, an Olympic Gold Medalist, and he pointed out that competitive right-handers did this too and he had pictures to prove it. I had always been taught in the old days that one kept that right elbow locked in, but I was astonished to find that the matter is really not critical. Today, most high-quality bolt-action rifles are available in both right- and left-hand versions, so the issue is not as significant as it used to be.

It is important to the morale of the novice to learn that superior marksmanship is by no means necessarily a function of superior eyesight. It is also comforting to those past their middle years to realize that one can keep shooting, and keep shooting well, even as the lights dim. Naturally, you cannot shoot if you are blind, but you have to be pretty far down that lonesome road before you become a total noncombatant.

Incidentally, there seems to be no truth to the rumor that blue- or gray-eyed shooters have an advantage over those with dark eyes. Somebody once discovered that blue-eyed shooters in the service out-shot brown-eyed shooters by a factor of six to four. This was considered important until it was discovered that the ratio of eye color in the services, irrespective of marksmanship, was the same. As recounted in the old vaudeville joke, "The white horses eat more than the black horses—because there are more of the white horses."

11

THE SHOOTING
SLING

The rifle sling serves two purposes: a carrying strap and an aid to steady holding. The simple carrying strap need not concern us here, because its function is transportation rather than marksmanship, but the shooting sling is another matter. It was given much attention back in the days when individual military riflemen were expected to hit individual targets, but since the adoption of the semiautomatic battle rifle generally throughout the world, it has rather faded from view in the public sector. This is not to say that we did not give it much thought when it was fitted to the mighty M1 Garand rifle, but during World War II the concept of precision rifle fire gradually faded, and the additional support given to the shooter by a proper shooting sling was in large measure forgotten. George Patton, for example, had no use for it; he felt that the infantry assault was characterized by the "fire storm" in which large numbers of men placed area fire upon an enemy position without primary concern for killing individual enemies.

I did all my early rifle shooting in the ROTC, National Guard, and Marine Corps utilizing the shooting sling, and I learned to make good use of it. In the hunting field its usefulness will depend upon the type of hunting undertaken. In the Pennsylvania woods or in the high grass of Namibia, it is rarely useful. On the other hand, when hunting mountain sheep, caribou, gemsbok, or pronghorn, the shooting sling can make a big difference. Though one man's experience may not be a proper basis for evaluation, I have hunted widely across the world, and I have used the loop sling in the field more often than I have not. It is no use whatever from the offhand position, but if you have time to assume a more stabilized stance, proper use of the loop sling will increase your likelihood of hitting by about 30 percent.

The function of the shooting sling is to take the weight off the muscles of your support arm, so that when you are in a proper firing position you can relax all your muscles and the weapon will remain exactly on target. This is accomplished by binding the support hand to the fore-end of the rifle and then securing that contact to the support shoulder so that the left elbow is held in its flexed position by the strap itself without any support from the biceps. This works when the support elbow is resting on something solid or something nearly so, such as the ground or the support leg; thus, it works in the prone, sitting, military squat, and kneeling positions—in addition to a good many "jackass positions," which may be improvised in the field.

You must always use the loop sling if you have time to get into it (provided you are not shooting from a rest and that your left elbow is supported).

Until recently the military loop sling, as issued by and taught by the U.S. armed forces, was the best thing of its kind, and it served its purpose very well. Its only drawback was time. It takes about five seconds to get into a military sling from a condition of unreadiness, and it is awkward to loop up while you are doing something else, such as leaping down from a truck bed or sprinting through the underbrush. In recent decades the principle of the CW sling has been rediscovered, and its modification known as the Ching Sling is now the preferred

With practice, the Ching Sling, shown here, can be mounted in a little more than one second.

device for the serious shooter. In every case the length of the strap must be adjusted to the build of the shooter, and a little time must be devoted to fitting the device to the individual who is to use it.

If one rifle is to be used by two or more people, much bother can be saved by the use of quick-detachable sling fittings, permitting each shooter to adjust his own sling and to snap it on when he takes over the weapon.

The military loop sling is put on as follows:

Step 1   With the left hand, turn the loop toward you, giving the strap a half-turn, and hold the loop open with the little finger of the shooting hand.

Step 2   Standing in the standard ready position, with the butt on the belt and holding the weapon in both hands, release the left hand and thrust it into the arm loop from left to right, spreading the loop with the fingers.

Step 3   Thrust the left arm through the loop from left to right as far as it will go, placing the loop well up into the left armpit.

The left arm is thrust through the loop as far as it will go . . .   *. . . and placed as high up on the upper arm as it will go.*

The left hand is then swung out to the left around the strap.   *Obtaining a practically instantaneous lockup.*

Step 4 Seize the rifle with the left hand while sliding the loop keeper firmly down onto the loop and thus holding it in place. (It is important to keep that loop as high up on the left arm as possible; otherwise it cannot support the weight of the weapon when the elbow is placed on support.)

Step 5 Regrasp the weapon with the right hand and swing the left hand down, out, and around the sling strap, inserting it forward between the strap and the rifle.

With practice, the American military sling can be mounted in about five seconds.

Now the left arm is locked to the rifle, and if the left elbow is placed on something solid the weight of the rifle will be born by the loop up in the armpit of the shooter and prevented from falling forward when the muscles of the left arm are relaxed.

This procedure must be practiced until it becomes completely reflexive and calls for no thought on the part of the shooter. A good field marksman will always "loop up" whenever he expects contact. This is particularly true when topping a ridge, either walking or crawling.

Back before the discovery of what may now be called the "speed slings," I sought out a couple of Olympic competitors for their advice as to how they got into their sling straps when competing in the Nordic biathlon. Since my friends and I could only beat a five-second delay under the best possible conditions, I was astonished to hear the Olympians tell me they could loop up in one and a half seconds. Upon investigation, I found out how. The biathlon shooter wears a jacket into which the loop around his upper left arm is permanently fixed and sports a D-ring. When the shooter wants to loop up, he simply snaps the fitting on his strap into the D-ring and is ready to go. This system works, of course, but its application to field shooting is questionable.

(The origin of the speed sling as rediscovered comes from Guatemala. On one of the occasions when I was working down in Central America, I was the guest of Carlos Widmann, who showed me an old military rifle on which a sling loop was affixed in front of the trigger guard. Upon experimentation, it became clear that the trigger guard mounting was forward of the shooter's armpit when in shooting position, thus securing the leather forward of the base of support without the use of a military loop. When a nominal carrying strap is secured with both its terminals forward of the trigger guard, no keeper is necessary to lock the loop around the arm, because the weight of the weapon itself will maintain nonskid pressure on the strap when in position. This was a marvelous discovery for me, and I termed a sling used in this position "CW" after Carlos Widmann.)

To use a CW sling, affix the broad end of your carrying strap into the middle sling socket and then give this strap a half-turn to the right and affix it forward. Now if you stand at standard ready, all that is necessary for you to mount the sling is to thrust your left arm all the way through it, flinging the broad end of the strap up into your armpit and then swinging

On the first count, the strap is given a half turn to the left and maintained in position by the little finger of the shooting hand.

The left arm is then swung away from the weapon, around and over the strap, and in between the forearm and the forward sling attachment.

When the arm is thrust all the way in and the loop is placed as high on the arm as it will go, the rifle is stabilized by the left hand, while the right hand slides the keeper down toward the arm to form a tight lock.

The military loop sling is very stable and secure, but considerably slower than the CW or the Ching Sling.

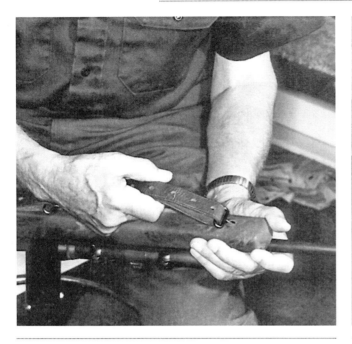

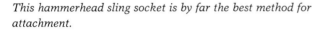

This hammerhead sling socket is by far the best method for attachment.

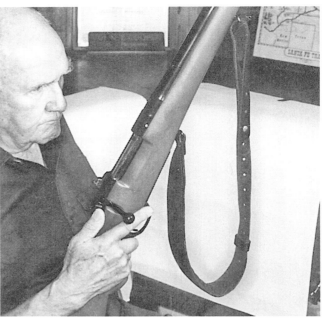

The CW sling in shooting mode.

your left hand out and around while maintaining pressure and thrusting your left hand between the rifle and the leather. You can do this in one second, and, furthermore, you can do it while you are engaged in doing something else, such as running, jumping, or going down into a stable firing position.

The speed sling may not be quite as stable for long strings of fire as the loop sling, because it is necessary for the shooter to maintain a degree of forward pressure on the band to keep it from sliding down toward the elbow. This is not a serious problem, however, and the experienced marksman can keep that loop up into his armpit as long as it is necessary to do whatever he needs to do in the field.

When I first began using the CW sling, I mounted it on the weapon in firing position as I took off on the hunt. It is not as comfortable a means of carrying the rifle as a sling mounted conventionally fore and aft. It works, however, and at the conclusion of the hunt it is easy to reverse it again, mounting the broad end

The CW sling in transport mode.

forward and the narrow end all the way aft for the long hike back to the truck.

In due course an improvement was introduced by Eric Ching, a multiple student at Orange Gunsite. He simply added an additional segment of leather between the loop and firing position and the rearward sling socket. This permitted the weapon to be carried in a conventionally slung position for hiking and yet instantly ready for mounting in the same manner as the CW sling. I have used this system now for many years, as have all of my friends and associates. If it is not as widely understood, marketed, and taught as it should be, that is probably because people have simply not been paying attention.

When practicing quick acquisition of firing positions, the shooter should begin looped up if he is using the military loop, but unlooped if he is using a speed sling. Only thus will he be able to take best advantage of his equipment.

The sling, of course, is of no use in snap shooting, nor does it do anything for the shooter who is using a bipod or other artificial rest.

When undertaking a close approach on dangerous game or checking out your backyard for intruders, the sling should be removed. Neither a sling strap nor a telescope sight will be of any help in a close encounter of the horrendous kind.

(*Note:* The so-called "hasty" sling technique is not the same as a speed sling.)

The skilled rifleman will always have the sling in place on his arm ready to go if he expects a chance to take a shot from a supported position. We should always be looped up when we "top out," because when we move up to the top of a rise we may sensibly expect that the increased vision available may show us something worth shooting. When mountain climbing, the hunter should always select a resting spot just short of the summit in which to get his wits about him, get his breath, and loop up.

It may appear that this is only valuable to the hunter, but McBride says that he often saw experienced infantrymen loop up in anticipation of a shot in the European theater of World War I.

12
BREATHING

Constructed as we are, humans have to breathe, but not necessarily during the second or two it takes us to press off a shot. The classic technique for breath control taught in military circles for well over a hundred years is thus: when you are in position and ready to fire, you take a deep breath, let it all the way out, and then inhale half a breath and hold that during the time you apply trigger pressure. This works well on the target range, and I see no reason to preach differently.

The time will almost certainly come, however, when the marksman will not have the leisure to control his breath precisely. Much of the time the field shooter is out of breath when he must take his shot. If possible, he avoids this by resting a few minutes before entering a situation in which he may have to shoot, especially in mountain hunting. This will not always be possible, though, and the shooter should understand that he can dampen the effect of heaving lungs, under most circumstances, and shoot pretty well in a hurry.

In an out-of-breath situation, the shooter simply tightens up as if he were going to receive a solid punch in the solar plexus. As his sights seek the target and his finger finds the trigger, he inhales hard and locks his muscles shut for a brief moment, which is enough for him to squeeze off a controlled shot. He then blows out quickly and inhales fully while operating the bolt and locks himself in tight for the second shot, should that prove necessary. This technique was explained to me many years ago by John Pepper of Maryland, who has conducted a great deal of practical rifle shooting on what may be called stress courses.

It is better, of course, to shoot only when one is calm and one's heart and lungs are relaxed, but if this is impossible, the shot is not necessarily lost. A late hit is better than a quick miss every time, and one of the important aims of practice is the determination by the shooter exactly what his own limitations are in this effort.

Legend has it that Bill Hickok accepted four misses on the part of his adversary Dave Tutt across the square in St. Joseph. According to the story he took the time and got the hit at what was an extravagant range for a pistol fight. One can never be sure of the accuracy of legends, but this tale can serve as a good example to us all.

13

THE SNAPSHOT

One is rarely called upon to use a rifle in a great hurry, since the rifleman normally takes the initiative. But there are exceptions, and one should know how to meet them. I will define the snapshot as one taken in two seconds or less from a condition alert but not aligned-in. The range is short, and the firing position is offhand. This stroke is not taught in any military organization of which I am aware, nor is it part of the training conducted by civilian schools. It is, however, one of the attributes of any completely qualified rifleman, and it is a very satisfying skill to command.

I have seen the snapshot used half a dozen times in the field, and I have had cause to use it three times myself. This suggests that the snapshot is not commonly encountered, and a preponderance of riflemen may go a lifetime without ever using it, but when one does need it, its execution is a marvelous comfort in that it is something like a pistol carried on the belt: one may go a lifetime without needing it, but when he needs it, he really needs it.

The firing position in the snapshot is offhand, and the offhand position should be learned at medium speed before the snapshot is attempted. This does not suggest slow-fire offhand—which is something of a contradiction in terms—but when in the offhand position, the shooter has time to correct his initial sight picture, he is not snapshooting.

An essential element of snapshooting is binocular vision. A right-handed shooter tracks with his left eye and shoots with his right. This takes a little practice, as it does not come naturally to most people, but the shift from the left eye to the right is readily mastered by anyone who knows what he is trying to do and puts a little time in on the effort. The snapshot may be accomplished with open sights, aperture sights, or telescope, but it is somewhat more difficult with open sights than with a ghost-ring aperture. An aperture sight (diopter) with a small aperture and a thick rim slows down the operation. Likewise, a telescope sight of high magnification and short eye relief tends to delay matters somewhat.

In practicing for the snapshot, the shooter assumes the standard ready position, foot alignment some 45 degrees to the right of his anticipated shooting direction. Although we cannot anticipate the circumstances under which the snapshot may be demanded, it is advisable to practice starting with the butt on the belt, thumb on the safety, and trigger finger straight outside the trigger guard. (An exception is the Garand-type action, in which the finger is within the trigger guard but off the trigger in contact with the rear of the safety switch.) In this position the muzzle of the rifle is held at eye level in the direction in which the shooter anticipates the target.

The call is "Eyes! Muzzle! Target!" On signal or at the initial appearance of the target, the rifle is mounted to the offhand position. Both eyes are wide open, and the safety is moved to the "ready." As the butt hits the shoulder, the finger finds the trigger, and with a two-stage military trigger, its slack is taken out. This calls for a little practice to avoid "going through" at the termination of the take-up. The rifle is pointed at the target as if the shooter were going to fire without sights, while both eyes remain open. The instant a correct

offhand position is assumed, the right eye takes over and acquires the sight picture on the target. If the rifle is mounted correctly, there will be no need to adjust. Pointing without sighting may not be easy at first, but practice will make it so. As the right eye takes over, finger pressure on the trigger commences, initiating the procedure known as the "compressed surprise break." A surprise break may be achieved in a split second, but the danger of the "duffer's pull" must be avoided.

Rather than telling your finger to press at a given moment, you must allow the weapon to "fire itself" within a very small interval to which you, the shooter, set the limits. This time interval may be so small as to be imperceptible to an observer, but you will know what you did, and you will be rewarded with a center hit if you do it right—and scolded with a miss if you do it wrong.

Starting from Condition 1 (cocked and locked), the count is simply, "One, two, three." Keeping both eyes on the target, on the count of one, you mount the rifle into the shoulder as you take the safety off and take the slack out of the trigger. One the count of two, you verify the mount by shifting your vision from left to right eye. When this is done properly, you will see your crosswires neatly quadrisecting your target the instant you make the change. Then, on the count of three, you achieve a quick surprise break, and all is well.

This exercise should be practiced at first without firing, but with complete concentration until the shooter's reflexes are properly programmed. It will take a little longer to master with the two-stage military trigger, but when this mastery has been achieved, the two-stage trigger has much to recommend it, as it effectively avoids the shot before the shooter is ready.

In practice, the shooter must make sure that the butt is solidly mounted into his shoulder on the count of one, as there is a tendency to drop the right elbow, engaging only the toe of the butt into the top of the shoulder.

This is the standard ready position when the shooter is expecting a snapshot.

This is the proper offhand firing position from the front and side. Note that the sling is not used, because the elbow is unsupported.

"Eyes! Muzzle! Target!"

As the piece is raised from ready, the safety comes off, the trigger finger finds the trigger, the butt finds the shoulder, and vision is shifted to the right eye.

In training, the snapshot is normally executed at intervals of one and one-half seconds, and a shooter is well qualified if he can place five consecutive shots in a four-inch circle at 25 yards, and in a ten-inch circle at 50. In my opinion, snapshooting is ill-advised beyond about 50 yards, because it is an emergency effort and does not allow the deliberation necessary for precise fire at middle to long ranges.

The snapshot should be practiced on paper until a degree of skill has been achieved—according to the stopwatch. At this stage, however, clay-bird shooting is an invaluable step forward. This does not mean that the competent rifleman should try deflection shots on flying targets, but that he should be able to mount his rifle and get off a controlled shot on a fleeting target in an interval that he can anticipate. Normally, the shooter stands next to the trap, and the bird is fired straight away from him. He mounts his rifle as the trap is sprung, tracking the clay target with his left eye while he points-in and picks up the crosswires with his right. The bird will be rising for a very brief time, and then, at the top of its trajectory, it will be apparently stationary for perhaps a second. During this time, the practiced shooter quadrisects the clay with his crosswires and achieves a surprise break before the bird begins to veer or descend. If the bird goes into deflection, hits will be mainly a matter of luck.

This clay shooting with a rifle is great fun, more so I believe than trapshooting with a shotgun since an accomplished trapshooter must go through a hundred rounds to find out if he has had a good day, whereas a rifle shooter needs only ten. A good shotgunner breaks well up to ninety birds out of a hundred,

or he is disgusted with himself. On the other hand, the rifle shooter has a good string if he breaks one out of ten. He is highly pleased with himself if he breaks two. If he breaks three out of ten, he runs the risk of overconfidence. With intense practice over a period, a really good rifleman can perhaps break 50 percent, but this is not to be expected on a normal day.

When two traps are available, excellent practice with bolt work can be achieved. In this exercise the second trap is sprung when the shooter fires, whether or not he hits. That means that he will snap that bolt instantly, butt to the shoulder, and then pick up the second bird. Any rifleman who breaks a double is good. Any rifleman who breaks a double twice can say that he understands the snapshot.

It may be asserted that snapshooting with a rifle is an affectation, because we are unlikely ever to have to hit a quail on the wing with our big-game rifle. Realism aside, however, anyone who does well on clay birds with a rifle has a confidence in his ability that gives him great comfort in the field. The finest shot I ever saw delivered was placed by the late Kerry Finn, of the Rhodesian Park Service, almost exactly between the eyes of charging buffalo at a range of about 30 steps. The record for clays stands at seven out of ten, achieved by a very feminine Orange Gunsite student from Alaska. The most spectacular string I ever saw was three in a row *on demand* placed by Russ Showers with an M1 rifle.

It is well to remember that most of your practice for snapshooting may be conducted with an empty weapon without going to the range. Your televisor will provide you with unlimited targets, and once you have tried the action with live ammunition for a few sessions, you will know in your own mind whether your dry shot was a hit or a miss.

14
WIND

Acrosswind will move a bullet's trajectory laterally if it is strong enough and the range is long enough. The effect of wind upon the projectile is a function of time; therefore, the longer the bullet is in the air, the more it will be moved by the wind. Consequently, average velocity—not initial velocity— over the entire distance is what will determine a bullet's movement by a crosswind. The shorter the time, the less the movement.

When shooting at extremely long range, as in old-fashioned military area fire, wind effect was an important element of musketry; thus it became a major factor in long-range target practice, especially at Bisley, the renowned rifle range out on the prairie in the south of England. At Bisley the course of fire took the shooter out to the extravagant distance of 1,000 yards. (As far as I know, it still does.) The wind never stops at Bisley, and the line of sight to the target is marked out by narrow, colored-cloth pennants at each 100-yard increment. When looking downrange, it is not uncommon to see those flags pointing in different directions at different ranges, and after the shooter achieves a certain precision in his prone position, his success or failure in the contest depends largely upon his ability to read those flags. This problem is equally present at any contest in which the shooters compete at maximum range, so "wind doping," as it is normally called, can be a very important element in a target shooter's repertoire. It matters very little in field shooting, where ranges are not usually long enough to be affected by wind and there are no pennants for the shooter's coach to read.

The better the ballistic coefficient of the projectile, the less it will be affected by wind, but the most important element in the coefficient is mass. Consequently, heavier bullets, if they are well-shaped, tend to be moved less by crosswinds than light ones.

Initial velocity helps to shorten time of flight at short range, but high velocity does not make up for ballistic efficiency as the range increases. For example, the 30-06 150 starting out with a 300 fps advantage at the muzzle over the 30-06 180, will be caught and passed by the latter at about 300 yards. When we note that the predicted velocity at that range is practically identical and remember that the 180 has a 20-percent edge in mass, it is clear that the impact effect will be greater at long range when a heavier bullet of similar ballistic shape is employed.

Thus it is that, contrary to what a good many people believe, the lighter, higher-speed bullet is better suited for short-range shooting than for long-range.

15
MOVING TARGETS

Only rarely will a rifleman be called upon to tag a target that is moving laterally across his front. Much more often his target will be moving straight away or straight toward him, and his shooting will not require deflection correction or "lead." Nonetheless, a shooter should not completely give up on running shots, especially in fighting, where sportsmanship is not involved.

Generally speaking, the hunter should pass up a running shot, but the soldier need not.

Using modern rifles of medium velocity at middle ranges, the time of flight from the bullet to the target is so slight that little deflection correction need be employed. The important thing is to make sure that the movement of the rifle in following the target is not checked at the moment of discharge—a common and usually disastrous error. When shooting at a target that is moving laterally across your front, you may hold dead center at short range, and lead by a hand's breadth or more as the range increases. However, you must keep your sights on the target as it moves, before, during, and after discharge. In shooting at moving paper targets, it is best always to fire two shots, working the action between them. This will tend to teach the shooter to keep his weapon moving as he shoots.

When shooting at a target coming straight in (for example, a charging lion), the shooter can treat the target as stationary. The target is coming straight, and the problem is not so much marksmanship as bullet placement. It is almost always a poor policy to shoot a fleeing creature squarely in the behind. (In Africa this is known as the "Portuguese Brain Shot.") One can think of exceptions, of course, particularly in the case of an animal that has already been wounded and may get away to die slowly, but a fleeing quadruped will nearly always run until it has distanced itself enough from what frightened it, to make it feel secure, and then turn sideways to look back and see what the threat was. Rarely will the animal hold that position long, so the shot will always be hurried, but it must be placed with great care and a cool head.

I was particularly pleased with one of my granddaughters when, on her first outing, she solved this problem exactly with her warthog. It was departing at top speed, but when she put the sight on it, all she could see was its rump. Quite properly, she held on target and waited. In a matter of 60 meters, the pig broke to the right and exposed its head at a target angle of about 145, whereupon she broke its neck with one quick, compressed surprise break.

16

ZEROING

A rifle is said to be "zeroed" when the line of sight of its sighting system coincides exactly with its average point of impact at a range selected by the shooter. A number of people who are not deeply instructed in firearms assume, first, that this condition is built in at the factory and, second, that once achieved, it will not change. This is not the case, and the achievement of a proper zero for any particular combination of rifle/sight/ammunition depends upon the shooter. We must realize that the shooter himself constitutes a "gun mount." He relates to his rifle exactly as the gun carriage relates to a field gun. When the piece fires, it moves and to a degree and in directions that are individually affected by the shooter's body.

Thus it is that one shooter can "zero" a rifle for another only by coincidence. For satisfactory results, you must zero your own rifle. The difference in point of aim between one shooter and another using the same weapon may be too slight to matter—but do not count on it.

Most modern rifles are accurate enough to be beyond criticism on the part of most shooters. This is not true, however, of the ammunition used. Ammunition variables are greater than one might expect, and I have known factory ammunition to show discrepancies of as much as 5 percent in the weight of the powder charge. If you want maximum precision in bullet placement from your rifle, you must either secure premium or "match-grade" ammunition or load it yourself—assuming that you are properly instructed in the principles of handloading.

It may be argued that theoretical precision is unimportant in the game fields or, for that matter, in a gunfight. There is enough truth in this to occupy our attention, but it is nonetheless very comforting to the rifleman to be able to prove for himself that the weapon, ammunition, and sighting system he has chosen are capable of placing every shot inside a bottle cap at the distance between the goalposts of a football field. He knows that he cannot shoot that well, but he likes to be serene in the assumption that pinpoint accuracy will help him shoot better. It will not, of course, but we all like to think that it will.

A rifle is ordinarily zeroed from a bench rest, which is a device intended to take as much of the human element out of shooting as possible while still permitting the shooter to control the weapon. (There is such a thing as a "machine rest," which does take the human element completely out of the operation, but it is both expensive and irrelevant to our study of marksmanship.) The bench rest is a desirable gadget, but in my opinion it has damaged contemporary marksmanship to a measurable degree. Far too many shooters believe that what they can do from a bench is what they can do in the field, and this, of course, is a fallacy. It is well to achieve a satisfactory zero from the bench before going afield, but it is not enough. The competent marksman will seek his field zero from a field position whenever he can.

In shooting from the bench the shooter first checks everything he can about his weapon. (An elemental safety precaution, of course, is to glance through the barrel to make sure that varmints have not made homes therein.) He should test all screws attaching the stock to the rifle, and the sights to the metal, to reassure himself that all contact is snug and consistent.

When ready to proceed he places the rifle on the bench so that the forward sandbag rest supports the piece where his left hand would if he were shooting without support. He then snuggles in behind the weapon and places the buttstock solidly into the meat of his shoulder, supporting it with the web of his left hand. Then he places his cheek on the comb in such a fashion as to obtain a clear view of the sight picture, whether unaided or assisted by telescope optics. He adjusts both front and rear support of the weapon to the point that, if he relaxes all outside pressure of right and left hand, the sights stay exactly on target. Normally, he adjusts for elevation coarsely by moving the forward sandbag and finely by adjusting the support of his left hand under the toe. He places his right hand on the firing portion of the buttstock, usually its pistol grip, and makes sure that this contact does not alter the sight picture resting squarely on target. Lastly, before applying any trigger pressure, he seats the buttstock firmly back into his shoulder with his firing hand. The support of the shoulder, and thus the body of the shooter, must be consistent, and consistency is best achieved by moderate, steady pressure of the butt into the shoulder. If the weapon is allowed to fly free on recoil, the inhibiting action of the shoulder and body will be uneven between shots.

When all is ready, the shooter drops the striker on an empty chamber with maximum care, to be sure that there is no apparent motion of the crosswire on the bull's-eye at ignition. He may then proceed by testing with live rounds.

It is desirable to zero your piece with the barrel in the condition you expect it to be in when you commence firing in the field. That suggests that the barrel should be wiped clean, but not oiled, for testing. There is a theory that the first shot from an oiled barrel

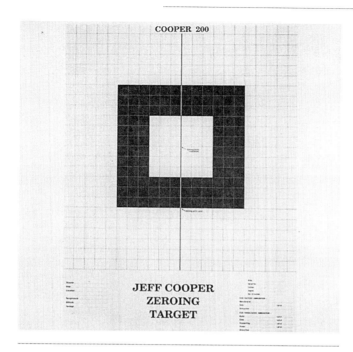

The zeroing target.

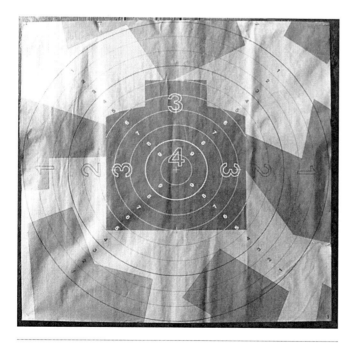

This is the Swiss qualification target on which every Swiss citizen must qualify annually. The 10 ring measures 10 centimeters in diameter, which is about four inches.

will throw high, and this sounds reasonable, but I have never been able to detect it personally. In some weapons the point of impact may shift somewhat as the barrel heats up. This ought not to be the case, but I have observed it in a couple of very high-priced custom weapons. If by mischance you own such a piece, it will be necessary to maintain the barrel in as cool a condition as possible between shots while zeroing, as this will delay impact shift considerably.

With an unfamiliar weapon I prefer to commence by firing at a pebble on the backstop while a companion observes the strike. It is not unknown for rifle and sight to be in such disaccord that your first shot may be clear off the paper and thus impossible to evaluate. If you can see the strike on a dirt bank, you can make broad corrections. If you do everything right that first shot should tell you much of what you need to know. As in artillery, it is desirable to make bold corrections, moving the point of impact clear across the point of aim, rather than trying to creep up on it. If you move your sighting dial a quarter-turn in the desired direction and find that moves your point of impact too far, it is then possible for you to come back to the point you desire economically by halving the distance on each round.

It is advisable to move your sights in only one plane at a time. Machinery being what it is, we frequently discover that when you wish to go right you may go up or down at the same time, simply because the mechanism of your sight is moving things in two planes at the same time.

Once you are on for deflection, it is time to adjust for elevation. With a beginner it may be desirable to fire two or even three shots before each adjustment, but an experienced hand can usually get on target one shot at a time without wasting ammunition.

It is not uncommon for a sportsman to attempt to zero at midrange, seeking a strike

THE ART OF THE RIFLE

about three inches high at 100 meters, for example. This ought to bring a medium-velocity combination into exact point of aim at 200 meters, which is a pretty good place to start for most rifles, most ammunition, and most shooters. However, this is not the end of the exercise. When you think you are on, it is time to set up a clean paper target and start again. A good procedure is to fire three shots as carefully as possible without observing the strike, either through a spotting telescope or by means of assistance from a friend. There is a definite tendency to try to make corrections in your hold if you know that you have made an error.

Correcting your hold comes later; now, we are trying to bring the rifle, ammunition, sights, and support into coincidence without your help.

It is best to commence with three-shot groups, using the mathematical center of the triangle as your reference point. Remember, however, that other things may enter into this process, and if you get two shots very close together, and one quite a way out, it may be the fault of the ammunition, especially if you did not "call" that shot out.

When you have achieved satisfaction at 100 meters, move out to 200. Extrapolation may satisfy under some conditions, but it is not the best procedure. With a rifle of moderate velocity—2,400 to 2,900 fps—200 meters is a good place to set your zero. This will enable you to hold as closely as your eyes permit on dead center out to about 250 meters. If you feel called upon to take a shot at 300, you will then have to hold a little high—300 meters is a very long way for you to make sure of your shot, despite what you may have read in the popular press.

If you are using a rifle of high velocity—3,000 fps or better—you may be content with a 250-meter zero. People who use their rifles for practice in the antipersonnel mode may desire to go farther than that. If your target is a humanoid silhouette, for example, you may be justified in zeroing for 400, remembering to hold low at shorter ranges.

Your test group at 200 should consist of five shots, each carefully called. The test group should be exactly centered on the point of aim, with "fliers" excluded as unrepresentative. (I have known some lots of military ammunition to throw one wild shot consistently out of group in twenty attempts. This is not common, but it should be acknowledged.)

When you have achieved a satisfactory five-shot zero at 200 meters, it is wise to move out to 300 to check your drop. You do not set your sights for 300, but you demonstrate just how far your particular load and combination are going to print below exact point of aim at that distance. If you have the facilities, this may be done by shooting at a rectangular steel plate some 12 to 14 inches in depth and placing the horizontal crosswire exactly on top of that rectangle.

Now for the last step. Move back to 200 and abandon the bench rest, shooting a very careful five-shot group from either prone or sitting position, utilizing the shooting sling. When you are absolutely sure of a killing shot from a field position at 200 meters, you are ready for the field.

Bear in mind that things can change. A hunting rifle should be verified at your hunting camp before setting forth to the horns. During an extended hunting trip, it may be well to verify at midterm. (I have had a telescope go completely askew right in the middle of a marvelous sojourn in the Okavango Delta.) It may be that the more expensive your glass, the less likely it is to change its mind in midcampaign. I am not sure of this, but there is an old expression to the effect that you get what you pay for.

17
RELOADING AND READINESS

The repeating rifle is normally carried afield in Condition 3, with magazine full and chamber empty. We may regard this as "normal" because in most hunting situations there is no need for an instantaneous first shot. Such circumstances do occur, however, and with these the rifle is carried with a full magazine, a live round in the chamber, and the safety on. Thus, when an instant opportunity presents itself, the safety is operated as the butt hits the shoulder and the slack, if any, is taken out of the trigger.

(There is some valid disagreement about this policy among experienced riflemen who maintain that reliance upon the mechanical safety is foolish and that the true "safety" of the piece is the trigger finger, which is properly kept outside the trigger guard until the shooter has his target in his sights. I find it hard to reject this, but I have been accustomed to Condition 1—fully loaded, hammer back, safety on—and I still continue to use the safety even in conditions of anticipated immediate contact.)

The expert marksman always reloads the chamber instantly after the shot, regardless of what he thinks he has achieved. If his target is down, he keeps it in sight long enough to be sure it will stay down. If it has disappeared from view, the marksman makes himself ready for instant contact as he follows up.

The self-loading rifle reloads itself automatically, as its name implies. However, the shooter of such a

When the shot is fired, the bolt is operated instantaneously without removing the butt from the shoulder. When this is done correctly, the shooter is back on target and ready for a second shot before his empty case hits the ground.

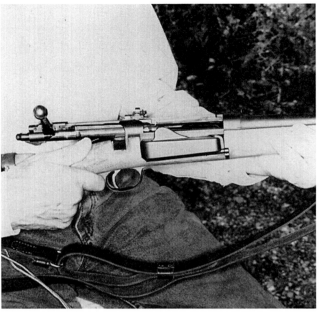

One of the unappreciated triumphs of the 19th century was the Krag rifle, whose action is still the smoothest and fastest to load.

piece must remember that his magazine must be topped off after each contact, which is best accomplished, of course, by replacing the magazine completely.

With the bolt-action rifle the shooter must program reflexive bolt work so that by choice the weapon is reloaded before the empty case hits the ground. My granddaughter Lisa illustrated this marvelously to all present on her first African kill. She did not need a second shot, but she did not think about that—she just snapped that bolt automatically. Having taught her this on the range, I enjoyed the bliss of the teacher when he sees his pupil performing perfectly.

There are those who feel that the bolt is operated in four stages: up, back, forward, and down. When done properly, however, this stroke has only two phases: back and forward. I have always tended to grasp the bolt knob between thumb and forefinger, but I have seen people execute it well with the palm of the hand. On

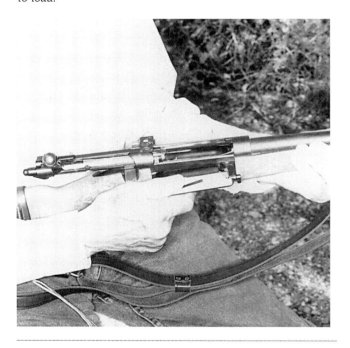

The magazine is snapped open with the thumb on the right side.

86

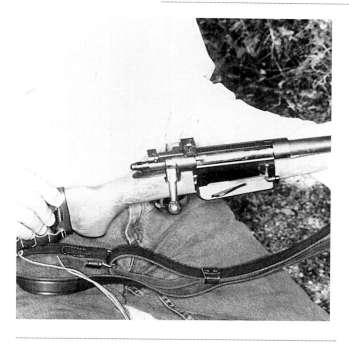

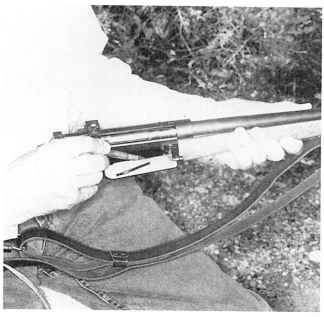

The spare round is produced from wherever is handiest . . .

. . . and snapped into the open action with no need for careful placement.

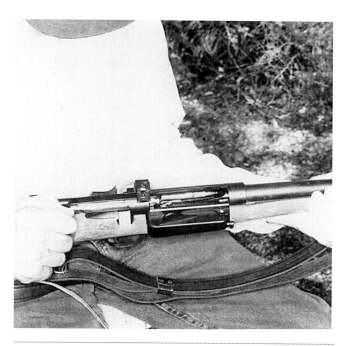

By this system, the rifle can be "topped off" without the shooter taking his eyes off his target.

some weapons there is not room between the raised bolt handle and the telescope for the thumb, and this makes the palm action necessary. Part of the merit of certain precision rifles is a very tight chamber, which makes the raising of the bolt difficult. A solution with these rifles is to place the shooting thumb on top of the telescope and the index finger beneath the bolt knob, allowing the shooter to pinch that bolt open with adequate force.

Bolt work should not be gentle. If a bolt is eased open, if may fail to extract; if it is eased forward without adequate retraction, it will not pick up the top round of the magazine.

I saw this happen on one occasion with a friend who had borrowed my heavy rifle for use on an elephant. The bolt-throw on this big gun was longer than he was used to, and when he did not retract the bolt all the way, he failed to feed as the bull's hindquarters collapsed, leaving him head-to-head with the shooter. My friend squeezed off his second shot carefully, but the piece did not fire because the chamber

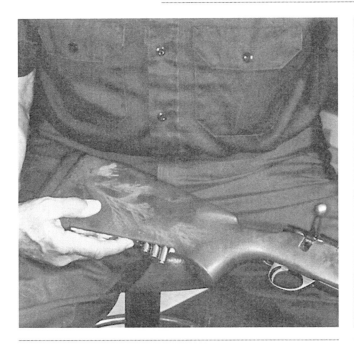

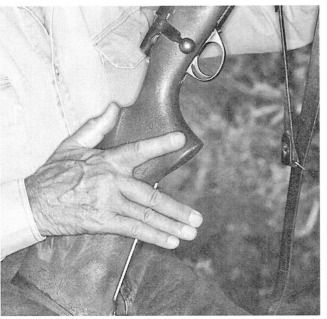

The butt magazine is a great convenience.

The butt magazine permits spare ammunition to be carried in the rifle and loaded very quickly with practice.

was empty. It has been said by Peter Capstick that the most terrifying sound on earth is not the whistle of a descending bomb nor the roar of a charging lion, but rather a click when we expect a bang. Do not let this happen to you. Work that bolt briskly!

With a lever-action gun a totally different system is employed. With such a piece the proper condition of readiness is Condition 3— magazine full, chamber empty. When mounting the piece, the first stroke is to move that lever down all the way, and then, as the butt is raised into the shoulder, the lever is closed back up in one easy motion. If you use a lever gun, practice that "one-two" mount until it is completely automatic—down on one and up on two.

With any sort of action, the principle remains the same: Do not take the butt out of your shoulder between shots! It astonishes me to find people who do not understand this, but I suppose such ignorance is because of the general adoption of the self-loading rifle for both military and sporting use. This phenomenon is somewhat akin to the general ignorance of the technique for

The cover is actuated with the second finger of the firing hand, allowing the thumb and forefinger freedom of action when the first round is discharged into the hand.

88

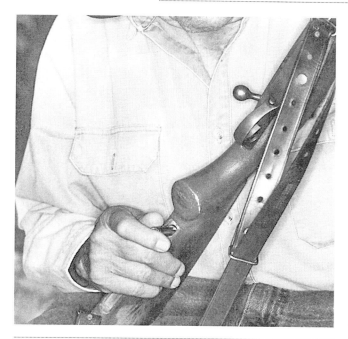

The spring-loaded ready round is thus popped briskly into the thumb and forefinger.

The bolt is opened with the little finger of the right hand, which then slips the ready round into the feedway.

If there are rounds in the magazine, they may be depressed slightly with the shooting fingers to avoid double-feeding as the bolt is closed.

This five-round butt magazine, designed and built by John Mahan of Chino Valley, permits the piece to be reloaded in a matter of two seconds with practice. It is particularly useful in jurisdictions that forbid rifles to be transported with loaded magazines. Five spare rounds in the butt, though not in the magazine proper, are very comforting in "night ready" situations.

A lever-action rifle is most conveniently carried in Condition 3 with no round in the chamber and the hammer down.

. . . and then the rifle is mounted to the shoulder as the lever is closed, thus the piece is loaded and made ready just as the butt hits the shoulder. This stroke is very efficient but not as widely understood as it might be.

When you are ready to shoot, the lever is forced vigorously downward to the extent of its stroke . . .

shifting gears on an automobile, since most cars now have automatic transmissions.

When practicing shooting from the offhand position, we should not forget to do some of the work with the rifle slung over the shoulder, both muzzle up in the American style and muzzle down in the African style. This technique must also be practiced when quickly assuming a stable position, either sitting or prone. A competent marksman should be able to start with the rifle slung, assume a stable position, and place two tightly controlled shots (in the black at 100 meters) in 10 seconds. This is a basic school drill.

With the single-shot rifle, the shooter loads as he goes into position, either from a carrier on his belt or from a butt-cuff or butt magazine on the rifle itself. This is quite a simple operation, and I have seen it carried out with "disconcerting alacrity," as the saying goes, but as with all other techniques, it must be practiced. It is unacceptable to take the field without practicing all these techniques until they are automatic.

18

THE MIND OF
THE RIFLEMAN

D uring the many decades I have studied, discussed, practiced, and taught rifle marksmanship, I have noticed that the state of mind of the rifleman is not a commonplace topic. I believe that this is a mistake, for if we agree that the purpose of shooting is hitting, the state of mind of the rifleman at the moment of discharge is probably the single most important element in success. This may be one reason why one occasionally encounters a mediocre target shot who is a particularly successful field shot. Target competition rewards consistency, as well it should, but in the field, either in hunting or in fighting, the ability to deliver the first shot is really all that matters. This ability is not so much a matter of eyesight, firing position, or trigger control as it is a matter of concentration. It seems apparent that the ability to concentrate on the task at hand is not uniform throughout the human race. Whether it can be taught, I am not sure; but I am sure that if you have it, you can become a superb field shot with only a modest amount of instruction and practice.

We often hear of a good shot, or rather a presumably good shot, who fails disastrously on that first round. Not long ago, an experienced federal officer, who has proven himself expert on the target range, told me that he felt that the several examples we have seen recently of egregious marksmanship in law enforcement work occurred because the participants were "excited," and if a shooter is sufficiently excited he cannot be expected to shoot well. This may indeed be true of some people, but it can never be true of the expert field marksman. At "the moment of truth," whether shooting at a paper target, distant antelope, charging buffalo, or human adversary, it is simply not acceptable for the shooter to let the excitement of the moment interfere with his sight picture and trigger squeeze. What this takes is concentration, the most important element of the exercise. The shooter must be able to block every extraneous consideration out of his mind. He absolutely must not allow the stress of circumstance to interfere with his shooting stroke in any fashion. The circumstances may be extremely exciting, before the shot and afterwards, but at the moment of the shot, there must be no room in the shooter's mind for anything but the technique of a perfect release.

I once heard it explained to me that the way to develop this was to sit quietly and alone, holding a kitchen match in your hand. If you can concentrate fiercely enough on that kitchen match to cause it to burst into flame eventually, you have achieved the proper level of concentration. Those of you who have cats in your household will note that a cat opens a closed door by concentrating on it. If he sits and concentrates on that door long enough, someone will open it. Lest we get carried away by arcane matters of extrasensory kinesis, however, we should get back to the practical point that it is concentration that secures the hits.

When I recently conducted our senior granddaughter on her first big-game hunt, this struck me forcibly. She was a good shot with the 30-caliber rifle. I had trained her myself, and I knew just how good she was. She was not the best in the class, but she could certainly be considered qualified. However, in the field she shone like the evening star. She took five trophies easily, cleanly, and with no apparent stress. One does not put down a zebra with one shot from a 308, but she did. One does not deck a blue wildebeest way over on the far mountain with one shot, but she did. A warthog is not difficult to kill, but it is hard to hit when it is running at top speed, as she did. And then there was the baboon way over on the distant cliff, well outside what I would call a sensible range. She put forth complete concentration, held two diameters high, and dropped him into the gorge below. This is concentration. Without proper technique, of course, it is not enough, but when coupled with proper technique, it is devastating.

"But I was excited!" This is not an acceptable statement on a part of a good shot. Self-control is what makes a good shot. Self-control is also what makes a good man. The two ideas are not necessarily coincident, but there is a connection.

19

THE MYSTIQUE OF THE ONE-SHOT KILL

To kill cleanly and painlessly with one round is a worthy goal that should be pursued by every conscientious rifleman. Like many such objectives, however, it may be carried to extremes. If the rifleman shoots long enough, there will come a time when his target is hit squarely, but refuses to react properly to the lethal blow. The field shooter must be instantly ready with his second shot, if needed, and it is up to him to be ready. In hunting big game, your target is never secured until you have touched him, and one of the serious weaknesses commented upon by African professional hunters in their clients is a tendency to "admire one's handiwork." You must never shoot, watch your animal drop, open your bolt, and look around waiting for applause. (I know. I speak from embarrassing experience.) In a much earlier episode I handled the matter wrong, but I lucked out, as will sometimes happen. This was up in the Canadian Rockies, where I had taken three prime trophies with three shots—with the 30-06 180. The fourth beast in sequence was a really impressive moose—he took first prize in the Clarke Contest that year. I had a solid position, using a horizontal rest at a range of about 90 paces. I put the shot where I intended, though picking out the spot was somewhat perplexing, since the shoulder of a moose is a big target and leads one to speculate about just where inside that huge body the most vital organs may lie. At the shot, nothing happened at all. I snapped the bolt, took up the slack on the military trigger, and waited, hoping fervently for a score of "four for four," and I waited. After an unreasonable time, the bull picked up his left knee, flexing it as it he had a stitch in his side, and put it down again. I should have put the second shot in, but I did not. I waited. Then, finally, the beast gently tipped over to his right and crashed to the ground with a shock that shook the forest. It was, indeed, four for four, but it might not have been. Luck was with me.

Ross Seyfried, the distinguished marksman who put in four years as a PH up in what is known now as Zambia, once told me to be very sure with a lion, above everything else, to keep on shooting. The one-shot kill is very nice to have in your log book. Enjoy it if it comes your way, but do not let its pursuit interfere with your success.

In the rifleman's war, he does not concern himself too much with niceties, being preoccupied with the problem of maintaining a whole skin. Nonetheless, the frequency with which the combat rifleman can deck his adversary with one round is a good measure of the combat efficiency of his unit. There have been few occasions in war wherein riflemen shot well. On two occasions that I can call to mind—Majuba Hill and Chateau Thierry—the results were devastating. Well-aimed rifle fire, when it can be achieved by infantry, is totally demoralizing.

20

TESTING AND THE EVALUATION OF MARKSMANSHIP

I t is impossible to define good marksmanship precisely because the rifle may be called upon to perform so many different tasks, and outstanding performance in one area may be meaningless in another. Nevertheless, we try to construct shooting exercises that will, in some measure, define a good shot. Over the decades in which I have been teaching rifle marksmanship, I have been subjected to dozens of different sorts of evaluations, and I have observed scores more. Every little bit helps, of course, but I feel that the standard evaluation exercises that used to be employed at our ranges at Gunsite could serve to measure with some accuracy the skill of the practical rifleman. We used to run these tests on the last day of a six-day course of rifle instruction involving the expenditure of about 360 rounds. Those students who excelled on these courses of fire may indeed be characterized as good shots.

OFFHAND

The snapshot is not well understood by most riflemen, and, in truth, it is seldom required in the field. I have used it on three occasions, and I have seen other people do so on perhaps half a dozen more. Rarity, however, does not constitute negligibility, and although you may never really need to use a snapshot with your rifle, if the occasion arises, you will really appreciate its skillful execution. As with the defensive pistol, you may never need it, but if you need it, you will really need it.

Having been an active rifle shooter for most of the 20th century, I consider that the finest shot I ever saw delivered for blood was executed by the late Kerry Finn in the late, great country of Rhodesia. A bull buffalo had been solidly hit twice, and, discovering as he ran that life was ebbing, he spun to charge. Kerry and I were both running through thin bush, but Kerry was the one who confronted the buff. Slamming to a dead stop from a dead run, Kerry planted a single round from his 470 exactly between the buff's eyes just as he commenced his charge—at a range of just under 25 paces. Kerry was later killed in action in the Rhodesian War, but his memorial is that buffalo skull that adorns a terrace of our home in Arizona. That half-inch hole squarely placed on the frontal bone of the skull is a lasting memorial to a master shot.

We test the ability of the aspiring riflemen to deliver the snapshot with consistency. The standard test is conducted at 25 and 50 meters, utilizing the IPSC Option Target, which includes a four-inch head ring and a ten-inch chest ring. At 25 meters, the shooter stands at standard ready, butt on hip, safety on, and muzzle aligned exactly between the shooter's eye and the target. At 25 meters, the target is the head ring, and the shooter is allowed one and one-half seconds to mount his rifle and deliver the shot. Not many men can place all five shots in that head ring every time on demand.

After firing five individual shots on signal at 25 meters, the shooter moves back to 50, where he engages the same target, but this time shooting for the 10-inch chest ring. The problem is the same and the time is the same, but the range is doubled and the scoring ring is larger.

I have always found the 50-meter stage to be slightly easier than the 25, but the rare shooter who can fire a perfect score with 10

successive shots, at one and one-half seconds from ready, has the right to be pleased with himself. Lest he become overconfident, however, he should repeat this exercise three times on three successive days before patting himself too hard on the back.

RIFLE TEN

For this test we also use the IPSC Option Target, placed at 300 meters. There are five firing points, one each at 300, 275, 250, 225, and 200. The shooter stands clear of his firing point, loaded as he pleases but unslung and with bipod, if any, folded. On signal, he dives into position—any position he may choose—and engages his target with two shots; after which, without signal, he is free to sprint forward to the firing point at 275, where he also fires two shots. He then moves to 250 for two shots and on to 225 for two shots. All firing positions are freestyle, and the shooter reloads without signal. After firing his pair at 225, the shooter must move forward to 200, where a chest-high screen forces him to shoot his two final shots standing erect. Time is taken from his starting signal to his last shot.

The IPSC Option Target has a 10-inch center ring. All shots in the center ring count five. Shots within the outer ring, but not in the X-ring, count four. Shots on the paper, but not within the rings, count two.

The maximum score is 50 points, and "par" time is 2 minutes. Any shooter who scores more than 40 points, with half of his shots in the X-ring, in 120 seconds or less, can consider himself a good shot.

(Coaches who wish to use this test for competition must take measures to ensure that the last two shots from the standing position are not wasted. A "gamesman" may deliberately throw away his two shots from offhand in return for a good time. In competition, this may be prevented by giving him another target at 200 and requiring that he get both shots on the paper or lose half his score.)

At a demonstration in Sweden, I once fired a score of 44 points on a Rifle Ten in a time of one minute 58 seconds, which pleased me very much. Imagine my distress when I read in the newspaper the following day that I had run the course in *58 seconds*, the journalist having simply dropped the minute. This news account made me out the greatest liar in Scandinavia, a title I am still trying to live down.

THE RIFLE BOUNCE

On this exercise we use the field target known as the Pepper Popper (invented by John Pepper). This is a slightly reduced semihumanoid steel target pivoted at the bottom and designed to go down to the shot when hit solidly. Its center ring measures eight inches in diameter, but this is topped by a head silhouette, which makes the entire target 22 inches high. It should be calibrated so that a head shot or a body shot will drop it but a shot in the knee will not.

Three firing points are set up adjoining, so that the shooter must reposition himself for each target. He starts at standard ready, unslung and with bipod (if any) folded. His three targets are placed at 100, 200, and 300 meters. On signal, he engages them in sequence. Firing positions are freestyle, and the shooter may fire at any target as much as he wishes as long as he does not exceed his six allowed rounds.

When he flattens his first target, he moves to his second firing position and engages his 200-meter target. When that is down, he moves to his third firing position and engages his 300-meter target. The object is to knock all targets down in the shortest possible time.

The system I find most useful for this is to take the short target from offhand, the middle target from the "rice paddy prone," and the long target from the prone position, but I do not hold the record. Younger men have cut the time down to the neighborhood of 15 seconds, but anyone who cleans the course in 20 seconds is good—especially if he can do it twice in a row.

This test is simple to administer and easy to score, there being no index other than elapsed time. (If a shooter cannot flatten all three targets with six shots, he receives no score.)

SUMMARY

The three foregoing simple tests do not constitute the entire range of rifle marksmanship, but they will serve to evaluate general rifle skill in a satisfactory manner. It will be noted that in every case accuracy is balanced against speed, because this balance is the essence of the activity. These tests do not involve pinpoint accuracy at extreme range, which is an attractive paper exercise but largely unrelated to the field use of the rifle.

Anyone who can do well consistently on these three tests, using a major caliber rifle, is a marksman to be taken seriously.